The Dragon's past, present and future

The

DRAGON

and the

WORLD

IS IT POSSIBLE FOR THE WHOLE WORLD TO BE DUPED?

Phil Hinsley

authorHOUSE®

AuthorHouse™
1663 Liberty Drive
Bloomington, IN 47403
www.authorhouse.com
Phone: 833-262-8899

Published by AuthorHouse 02/16/2024

ISBN: 979-8-8230-2245-3 (sc)
ISBN: 979-8-8230-2244-6 (e)

The

Dragon

and the

World

2024

Author's note

Somehow I had written two versions of this book, and that was in 2012. Since then I went on with other things and only recently rediscovered them and had to decide which of the two I would work on. In the end I thought that both had ingredients that were worth keeping so what you have has been culled, edited and rewritten from two sources along with new material which I hope makes for a more interesting read.

Also by Phil Hinsley

Wolves in sheep's clothing

Aspects of God

Contents

Introduction

The Dragon

I was born in the land of dragons. We could all see them. They were everywhere, fierce, strong and destructive. They flew above our heads and became almost commonplace.

They were never a threat to us; they were our protectors; the dragon was ours and we were his. They were a dramatic sign, but now they were inactive and rarely moved, yet there was one who instilled in me a shiver of fear. He seemed more real than the others. He stood guard outside the City Hall in Cardiff, as a reminder of earlier times when it was called Y Ddraig, Goch, The Red Dragon.

Romano-British soldiers carried the banner of the red dragon (Draco) to Rome in the fourth century. The standard bearer of the cohort was called draconarious. It was a symbol of power and authority. Ancient Welsh leaders went to war with its image on their battle standards. The dragon is also linked with Arthurian legends. Uther Pendragon's name translates as Dragon Head.

In 1138 the Scots used it as a royal standard. Richard 1 used it, as did other English kings. It was seen at the battle of Agincourt and was carried by Henry Tudor after the battle of Bosworth Field into St Paul's Cathedral. It was around that time that the green and white background was added to the flag.

Why would kings use such a symbol? What was this allegiance to? Churchill called it, 'an odious design expressing nothing but spite, malice, ill-will and monstrosity?' Did they want this red dragon to lead them and were they the red dragon's subjects?

Could it be more than just a symbol on a cup or teacloth, or raised high on flags? Does it perhaps represent something that is unseen yet very real and of great power whose influence has left none of us untouched? Many will say, No it's just a symbol. I'm not deceived, or duped, others are, but not me, I know what's true'. Yet the dragon that is described in the bible began his dark work long before humans were on the earth. But who believes that?

I grew up in Barry, South Wales. In the late 1800s the town was rich in the diversity of its nonconformist chapels and they combined in the fight against immorality and drunkenness. The National Vigilance Association (which was formed in 1880 to expose the traffic in innocent English girls to the continent for a life of prostitution) held crusades against the growing social evils that appeared alongside the new dock developments. There is an impressive sculpture in front of what was the General offices of Barry Railway Company of David Davis holding open a plan of the new docks in his hands. It was made by Alfred Gilbert who also made the Shaftesbury Memorial Fountain at Piccadilly Circus which is topped by Eros. According to Richard Dorment, who wrote a book on Gilbert, 'He is in fact Anteros, Agape, the embodiment of selfless love.'

The Temperance movement in Barry was also active through the town council in banning all premises that sold alcohol. The Rev L. Ton Evans said, 'Immorality was due to the deplorable sin of drunkenness.' There were no pubs so those who wanted a drink went to the hotels, as a result very few were able to obtain their licence. The Barry Dock Hotel, in Holton Rd, very close to where we lived, was converted into The Voluntary Hospital for the Destitute Sick and Dying as it failed to obtain a licence. The local Free Church Council and Temperance Societies continued to organise campaigns to persuade public opinion to oppose new licences for hotels and law-abiding citizens were urged to assist the police by volunteering information and evidence.

As a skinny blond kid in the mid-fifties, who wasn't interested in where I could get a drink stronger than cream soda, Barry had all I wanted. Not only the long sandy beach and the vividly painted rides of the fairground but more importantly for me the four cinemas, not counting the one in Cadoxton, which I only went to once as it wasn't in my part of town. There was the Romilly, The Theatre Royal, the Tivoli and the Regal where I saw the first Cinemascope film, 'The Robe'. There are no cinemas in Barry today.

When I wasn't in one of these cinemas, I was usually outside studying the posters and photos of next week's films. It was a great day for me when Gladstone Secondary Modern school for Boys emptied and this long line of boys and teachers snaked its way down to the 'Rom' to see the epic 'The Ten Commandments', which, like all films then, was in a square format. We walked up the broad stairs to where the tickets were sold and saw Life-size cut-outs of the stars of the film standing around the foyer – they would be worth something now.

Perhaps the school thought this biblical story might have some edifying effect on us but for me it was an escape into another world of wonder, helped by Elmer Bernstein's score. The teachers slipped up next time when they took us out to see 'Henry V' and we were totally bored, including, I think from their expressions, the teachers as well.

Any little thought I may have had about Christianity had come from whatever biblical film I saw. When John Huston's film 'The Bible, in the beginning' came out I noticed that when Abraham, played by George C. Scott, started to pray he used the language of the 1611 Authorised Version of the bible which taught me that to pray correctly, not that I did, one had to speak by using obsolete words – God obviously preferred humans to speak to him this way and I found this consistently in all the biblical films I saw.

We can learn a lot of theology from films – it wouldn't be correct, but it would look convincing. The great adventure film 'Raiders of the lost Ark' isn't intended as a biblical film yet there are scenes where the bible is referenced which many might think as an accurate retelling of the stories found in those old texts. There's a scene early in the film where Indiana Jones and another professor are explaining to two American secret agents what the Ark of the Covenant was used for, because the

Nazis were searching for it so the authorities in the west needed to know why.

Conveniently there was a huge old bible with clasps on the table and Jones opened it at a page where there was an illustration of priests holding poles that slotted through four golden rings on each corner of the ark and in this picture rays of light were emanating from it and the enemy were falling dead. The ark was being used as a weapon of mass destruction and Jones says, or perhaps it was the other chap with him, 'It could level mountains and lay waste whole regions' and then Jones adds, 'That's what the bible says', and then says, 'the ark contains the broken remains of the stone tablets that the ten commandments were written on.'

Later in the film, set somewhere near Cairo, Jones meets his adversary, a fellow archaeologist named Belloc who's working for the Nazis. Jones believes his girlfriend has just been killed so he's in no mood for a polite chat. They sit at a table and Belloc says, 'We've got a lot in common – archaeology is our religion, yet we've both fallen from the pure faith,' he goes on to say, 'Do you realise what the ark is? It's a transmitter, it's a radio for speaking to God, and it's within my reach!'

'You want to talk to God?' snarls Jones, 'Let's go see him together – I've got nothing better to do,' he reaches for his gun, but he sees all types of weapons suddenly pointing his way, just then he's quickly ushered out by a friend.

It's one of the great films of Spielberg but of course none of it is true. Moses didn't put broken pieces of the ten commandments in the ark – the ark was not a radio for talking with God and the ark wasn't a WMD.

Some films attempt at a more serious depiction on biblical stories such as a series some years ago called, unimaginatively, 'The Bible' where two angels are sent to Sodom to rescue Lot and his family and we see that they are excellent sword fighters – perhaps the producers felt the biblical account a little boring. Another series was called 'The Red Tent' and told the story of Jacob and his sons seen from the point of view of his daughter, Dinah. Unfortunately they left out the bible altogether, apart from the names.

The film I most keenly waited to see was Mel Gibson's 'The Passion'. This film was applauded by many Christians who used it as an effective evangelical tool yet, for me, it was a personal view from a director who favours the Catholic Church prior to Vatican II. This has to do observing the Tridentine Mass, all in Latin, which was codified in 1570 and reformed in the 1960s. There was a lot of emphasis in his film on blood and more blood, comparable to a Hammer horror film, and we see Saint Veronica and her cloth, who isn't mentioned in the New Testament. But not many seemed to mind.

Part 1

The Enemy

A woman was pregnant and cried out in pain as she was about to give birth. Unseen by anyone present was an enormous red dragon. The dragon stood in front of the woman who was about to give birth, so that he could devour her child the moment it was born.

This horrific scenario appears in the opening section of the twelfth chapter of the last book in the bible; Revelation. The child was born safely, it was a boy. His destiny is to rule all the nations. This part of the biblical text is left out of the sanitised Christmas stories that, for convenience sake, have the wise men at the stable when in reality they came much later, and there were more than three and it wasn't in winter time.

Her child was snatched up to God and to his throne. Nothing is mentioned of his life, death and resurrection but returns to the woman who now, in this highly symbolic writing style, becomes the persecuted church that escapes into the desert, which could represent the spiritual wilderness of this world, to a place prepared for her by God, where she might be taken care of for 1,260 days. This reoccurring time period is also given as time, times and half a time and forty-two months which represent the time between Jesus' first coming and his second. This same time period is found in Daniel 12:7. They all refer to a 3½ years period. How are we going to understand these odd time periods? It could be that this 3½ years is code for the creation of the new Israel; the church – from its inception to Christ's return, just as his ministry was about the same time period. We are not given the date of his return but we are given a symbolic number - 3½ years.

The text, Revelation 12:5, moves from newborn baby to world ruler in one verse. He will remain in heaven until the time comes for God to restore everything, as he promised long ago through his holy prophets, Acts 3:21.

Eugene H, Peterson, in his book 'Reversed Thunder' give us some valuable principles in reading the book of Revelation.

'The Revelation has 404 verses. In those 404 verses, there are 518 references to earlier scripture. If we are not familiar with the preceding writings, quite obviously we are not going to understand the revelation … there is probably not a single Old

Testament book to which he doesn't make at least some allusion … The statistics post a warning: no one has any business reading the last book who has not read the previous sixty-five. It makes no more sense to read the last book of the Bible apart from the entire scriptures than it does to read the last chapter of any novel, skipping everything before it. Much mischief has been done by reading the Revelation in isolation from its canonical context. Conversely, the Revelation does some of its best work when it sends its readers back to Genesis and Exodus, to Isaiah and Ezekiel, Daniel and the Psalms, to the Gospels and Paul. St. John did not make up his visions of dragons, beasts, harlots, plagues, and horsemen out of his own imagination; the Spirit gave him the images out of the scriptures that he knew so well; then he saw their significance in a fresh way. Every line of the Revelation in mined out of rich strata of scripture laid down in the earlier ages … In these 518 references to earlier scripture there is not a single direct quotation.'

We need to rid our minds (as John Stott has written) of the medieval caricature of Satan. Dispensing with the horns, the hooves and the tail, we are left with the biblical portrait of a spiritual being, highly intelligent, immensely powerful and utterly unscrupulous. Jesus himself not only believed in his existence, but warned us of his power. He called him 'the prince of this world' much as Paul called him 'the ruler of the kingdom of the air'. He has therefore a throne and a kingdom, and under his command is an army of malignant spirits who are described in scripture as 'the powers of this dark world' (What Christ thinks of the Church, p.50).

We do face a real enemy whose aim is to destroy us. In the light of this, Paul says to the Ephesians, 'Finally, be strong in the Lord and in his mighty power. Put on the full armour of God so that you can take your stand against the devil's schemes. For our struggle is not against flesh and blood, but against the rulers, against the authorities, against the powers of this dark world and against the spiritual forces of evil in the heavenly realms' Eph 6:10-12.

The devil can transform himself into an 'angel of light,' 2 Cor 11: 14, and he is a dangerous wolf, but enters Christ's flock in the disguise of a sheep. Sometimes he roars like a lion, but more often is as subtle as a serpent. His preference is to seduce us into compromise and deceives us into error. He plays both the bully and the beguiler. Force and fraud form his chief offensive against Christians.

Paul's letters were written to people who were previously 'foolish, disobedient, deceived and enslaved by all kinds of passions and pleasures. We, he wrote, lived in malice and envy, being hated and hating one another' Titus 3:3. Jesus' mission was 'to rescue us from the present evil age' Gal 1:4.

The only weapon that the Christian is given is a sword, the sword of the spirit, which is the word of God. But even good and sharp swords can be misused in the wrong hands and personal conviction does not always mean that it will be used wisely. In other words, the bible can and is used to mislead people.

Paul knew all too well that false gospels and false Christs were already taking hold of people's attention and these distortions were coming from those who looked and sounded more like apostles than Paul did. Paul wrote that he may not be a trained speaker but he did have knowledge and because of the love he had for the Corinthian church he was doing all he could to 'cut the ground from under those who want an opportunity to be considered equal with us in the things they boast about. For such men' Paul went on to say, 'are false apostles, deceitful workmen, masquerading as apostles of Christ. And no wonder, for Satan himself masquerades as an angel of light. It is not surprising then if his servants masquerade as servants of righteousness. Their end will be what their actions deserve' 2 Cor 11:12-15.

Deception was just as prevalent in Paul's day as it is in ours. 'I am astonished that you are so quickly deserting the one who called you by the grace of Christ and are turning to a different gospel – which is really no gospel at all. Evidently some people are throwing you into confusion and are trying to pervert the gospel of Christ. But even if we or an angel from heaven should preach a gospel other than the one we preached to you, let him be eternally condemned' Gal 1:6-8.

Paul was against all forms of deceit. 'We do not use deception, nor do we distort the word of God' 2 Cor 4:2, and deceit goes all the way back to the first contact between humans and the dragon.

In John's first letter we come across a very stark statement, which says, 'This is how we know who the children of God are and who the children of the devil are ...' 1John 3:10. John Stott, in his commentary on this section, writes, '... there are only two groups. There are not three. Nor is there only one. This 'very plain black-and-white' is not only true in itself, but also necessary ... God and the devil are irreconcilable opposites. Our parentage is either divine or diabolical. The universal fatherhood of God is not taught in the Bible, except in the general sense that God is the creator of all (Acts 17:28). But in the intimate, spiritual sense God is not the Father of all people, and not all people are his children. Indeed. John here is only echoing what Jesus once said to certain unbelieving Jews: 'You belong to your father, the devil' (Jn. 8:44, Mt 13:38, Acts 13:10).

This is not a call to point a critical finger at other churches but to look carefully at your own understanding because no one has been immune to this worldwide deception – to one degree or another.

In late February 1943 bright red posters were displayed in Munich. They announced:

Sentenced to death for High Treason:

Christoph Probst, age 24

Hans Scholl, age 25

Sophie Scholl, age 22

The Sentences Have Already been Carried out.

Inge Scholl, the sister of Sophie Scholl, has written, 'The newspapers carried reports of irresponsible lone wolves and adventurers, who by their acts had automatically excluded themselves from the community of the *Volk*. The president of the People's court, Roland Freisler, the notorious Nazi judge, had been flown in expressly from Berlin to execute swift judgement.

In a subsequent court action the following were also condemned and executed: Willi Graf. Professor Kurt Huber. Alexander Schmorell.

What had these people done? What was their crime?

While some people mocked and vilified them, others described them as heroes of freedom.

They stood up for a simple matter, an elementary principle: the right of the individual to choose his manner of life and to live in freedom. They did not seek martyrdom in the name of any extraordinary idea. They wanted to make it possible for people like you and me to live in a humane society.'

On a sunny Thursday, February 18, 1943, Hans and Sophie set out for the University of Munich. They had been able to pack a suitcase with leaflets. A few moments after they left the house a friend rang the bell, his mission was to give them an urgent warning, but he was too late and did not know where they were. When they arrived at the university they had only a few minutes before the lecture rooms were opened so they quickly decided to deposit the leaflets in the corridors, and they disposed of the rest by letting the sheets fall from the top level of the staircase down into the entrance hall.

They were about to go out when they were spotted by the building superintendent who immediately locked the doors and called the Gestapo. The fate of brother and sister was now sealed.

They were taken away and interrogated. All who were in contact with them – their fellow prisoners, the chaplains, the guards, and even the Gestapo officials – were deeply impressed by their bravery and the dignity of their bearing. After the second day of their detention it became clear that they must expect a sentence of death. Three had been arrested and they were determined to take upon themselves the so-called blame for everything, in order to lighten the burden of the others. The day of the trial came and Sophie the court appointed defence lawyer that 'If my brother is sentenced to die, you mustn't let them give me a lighter sentence, for I'm exactly as guilty as he'. She asked the lawyer whether Hans, as a soldier with service at the front had the right to execution by firing squad. To this question she was given an ambiguous reply. Her next question was whether she would be publicly hanged or would be executed on the guillotine. He was not prepared for that sort of question, especially from a girl.

Their parents travelled by train to visit their son and daughter in prison, with them was their youngest son, Werner, who had unexpectedly returned two days before on leave from Russia. They were told that there was not much time and they hurried to the Palace of Justice and made their way into the chamber where invited Nazi guests had been seated. There sat the judges in their red robes, Freisler in the centre, all fuming and sputtering in rage.

By the time the parents arrived the trial was nearly over. They were just in time to hear the sentences pronounced. The mother lost her strength for a moment and had to be escorted out of the room. A wave of excitement went through the room when the father cried out, 'There is a higher court before which we must all stand!' The mother quickly regained her composure and planned to draw up a petition for mercy and to meet her children. Werner made his way to the prisoners and took their hands. With tears welling in his eyes, Hans calmly laid his hand on his shoulder, 'Be strong, admit nothing.'

Each of the three was called upon in the customary way to make a statement at the close of the trial. Sophie said nothing. Christoph requested that his life be spared for the sake of his children. Hans supported Christoph's plea and put in a word for his friend, but Freisler brutally cut him off, saying, 'If you have nothing to say on your own behalf, please be quiet'.

The three were transferred to the large execution jail at Munchen-Stadelheim. There they wrote their farewell letters. The parents were able to meet them once more. Hans told them that he had no hatred and that he had put everything behind him. His father embraced him and said, 'You will go down in history – there is such a thing as justice in spite of all this'.

Then Sophie was brought in by a woman warden. She wore her regular clothes. Her mother said, 'So now you will never set foot in our house'. 'Oh, what do these few short years matter, mother', she answered. Then she said, 'we took all the blame, for everything, that is bound to have its effect in time to come'. Her mother wanted to give her daughter something she might hold fast to, 'you know, Sophie – Jesus,' Sophie replied, 'yes, but you too'. Then she left, still smiling.

Christoph was not able to see any of his family. His wife was not yet out of the hospital after the birth of their third child. She did not learn of her husband's fate until after the execution.

The prison guards reported that they bore themselves with marvellous bravery. The whole prison was impressed by them. They were brought together once more, just before the executions. A warden said, 'If our action had become known, the consequences for us would have been serious. We wanted to let them have a cigarette together before the end. It was just a few minutes that they had, but I believe that it meant a great deal to them'. 'I didn't know that dying can be so easy', Christoph said, adding, 'In a few minutes we will meet in eternity'.

'Then they were led off, the girl first ... the executioner said he had never seen anyone meet their end as she did'.

Hans, before he placed his head under the guillotine, called out, 'Long live freedom'. This was February 22, just four days after their arrest.

President Theodor Heuss of the Federal Republic of Germany spoke to the students of Berlin and Munich on February 22, 1953, saying:

'When, ten years ago we learned – first in the form of a rumour and later reliably confirmed – of the bold attempt of the Scholls and their friends to touch the consciences of university students, we recognised and stated: This cry of the German soul will echo through history. Death cannot now, nor could it then, compel this outcry to silence. Their words, sent fluttering on sheets of paper through the hall of the University of Munich, were and have remained a beacon.

The courageous death of these young people, who pitted integrity and courage to voice the truth against empty rhetoric and the lie, became a victory at the moment when their life was cut off. This is how we must understand their appearance in the midst of the German tragedy: not as an unsuccessful attempt to bring about change in the face of force, but rather as the extinguishing of a light shining in the darkest night.

For this we express our gratitude and honour their memory'.

These people protested against a great evil force of the 20th century – Nazism. But evil is still with us and there is never a shortage of tyrants, whether in homes or ruling nations. The dragon, who amplifies human evil, cannot be killed, only resisted. It is a spiritual war and we should be bold enough to speak up against the lies and misrepresentations he has caused to be taught, and have become, over a long period of time, some of the most commonly accepted beliefs of Christianity.

There is a number of books about Sophie Scholl available and the White Rose movement. I used a book from a school library so I had to return it and sadly don't remember the author's name. There is also a two-disk DVD about her.

Part 2

Genesis

T his earth has a pre-history that goes beyond Adam and Eve. There was life on earth before the first humans. Billions of years before our first parents large and predatory creatures covered the land and swam in the seas and flew in the air. Those that we know of have been given names such as spinosaurus, tyrannosaurs and megalodon – brought back to life in the films Meg 1 and Meg 2. This was not a world suitable for humans, especially if they swam. The recently excavated remains of a pliosaur was hardly friendly enough to be brought before Adam to give it a name, Gen 2:19-20.

Spirit beings oversaw life as it was then and in control was an awesome being of great beauty and splendour.

The prophets, Isaiah and Ezekiel, in writing of the king of Babylon and the king of Tyre, they turn from writing about a man to a being that is much more than a man. Isaiah 14:12 has, 'How you have fallen from heaven, morning star, son of the dawn.

You have been cast down to the earth, you who once laid low the nations. You said in your heart, I will ascend to heaven; I will raise my throne above the stars of God; I will sit enthroned on the mount of assembly, on the upmost heights of Mount Zaphon (the far north, see Psa 48:2). I will ascend above the tops of the clouds; I will make myself like the Most High.'

Turning to Ezekiel 28: 12b, we read, 'You were the seal of perfection, full of wisdom and perfect in beauty. You were in Eden, the garden of God; every precious stone adorned you … on the day you were created they were prepared. You were anointed as a guardian cherub, for so I ordained you. You were on the holy mount of God; you walked among the fiery stones. You were blameless in your ways from the day you were created till wickedness was found in you.'

This powerful being took his angels and made an assault on God himself (second letter of Peter and Jude mention this rebellion). That war caused cosmic ruin, not only on this planet, but on everything around it, as witnessed by our moon and on Mars. Verse two of Genesis describes the earth as 'formless and empty'. These words can also be translated as 'chaotic and in ruin'. And the word *was* could also be read as *became.*

God then renewed the earth creating vegetation, plants and trees. And the water, once more teemed with living creatures, and birds flew in the sky and all sorts of animals were created. Then God said, 'Let us (God was speaking to his divine council – spirit beings that God works with) make man in our image, in our likeness and let them rule over all the earth.

In the 1611 King James version, known as the AV, Genesis 1:28 has; And God blessed them and God said unto them, Be fruitful, and multiply, and replenish the earth, and subdue it ...'

Chapter 9:1 we read of the family of Noah after the flood, being told to, 'Be fruitful and multiply, and replenish the earth', just as Adam and Eve were commanded to do. The RSV and the NIV use the word fill instead of replenish but if we were to keep the word replenish, it's clear what it meant to Noah and his family. Whatever the word was that was said to Adam and Eve they understood its meaning. Many words used in 1611 do not have the same meaning today. So, 'fill' is a good translation and 'replenish' also conveys the meaning. There were no humans before that time and only eight people survived the flood.

'In the beginning God created the heavens and the earth'. Then comes a period of time that is not recorded and could be any number of years. Then we get to verse two and find a wasted, darkened and ruined world.

The dragon spoke to the woman, and the man was close by. The dragon is described as a snake, but consider a man who eats greedily. Someone might say to a man like that, 'you eat like a pig' or 'you're a pig' or just call him a 'pig'. The dragon is given several names that describe his character rather than being that particular creature. The dragon might have appeared as a reasonable man who you could talk to but his evil nature was just the same. Devil means 'the Slanderer' and Satan means 'Adversary'.

The enemy of God and humankind said to Eve, 'Did God really say, 'You must not eat from any tree in the garden'?' An obvious exaggeration, but one the woman would correct and add her own exaggeration into this conversation by saying that as well as not eating from this one tree, they must not touch it either, or they will die.

The 'serpent' reassured the woman that she would not die; it was just that God wanted to restrict what they could learn so he could better control them. But if they did choose to eat, he went on, they would have their eyes opened and come to know divine truth as God does.

The woman's interest was stimulated and she looked more closely at the fruit of the tree and saw that it was good to eat and it looked nice and she wanted to be wise so she took it and started to eat it. She passed it to her husband who had not said anything so far. He was not taken in by the 'snake' but he still went ahead and ate some as well.

Enlightenment, as the serpent promised, did come, but it was not the positive experience they had looked forward to. Shame, guilt and fear entered their lives, and they hid from the presence of God. When they were confronted with their disobedience they were quick to defend themselves by deflecting the blame onto someone else. The man blamed the woman and the woman blamed the serpent.

From then on their rule over the earth was ended before it had begun. It had depended on obedience to God, but they allowed themselves to be persuaded by the dragon masquerading as the voice of reason and lost their promised future. Their lives would now be characterised by pain and conflict. Each would try to dominate the other. There would be violence and corruption and mankind would look to those things around and above them for their beliefs, and their minds were darkened as they were led, unknowingly, by the dragon. It was his world and now they were his children.

Around 4,000 years later the apostle Paul wrote about the significance of Adam's sin and what it means for us today:

Therefore, just as sin entered the world through one man, and death through sin, and in this way death came to all people, because all sinned – To be sure, sin was in the world before the law was given, but sin is not charged against anyone's account where there is no law. Nevertheless, death reigned from the time of Adam to the time of Moses, even over those who did not sin by breaking a command, as did Adam, who is a pattern of the one to come.

'But the gift is not like the trespass. For if the many died by the trespass of the one man, how much more did God's grace and the gift that came by the grace of the one man, Jesus Christ, overflow to the many. Nor can the gift of God be compared with the result of one man's sin: the judgment followed one sin and brought condemnation, but the gift followed many trespasses and brought justification. For if, by the trespass of the one man, death reigned through that one man, how much more will those who receive God's abundant provision of grace and the gift of righteousness reign in life through the one man, Jesus Christ.

'Consequently, just as one trespass resulted in condemnation for all people, so also one righteous act resulted in justification and life for all. For just as through the disobedience of the one man the many were made sinners, so also through the obedience of the one man the many will be made righteous.

The law was brought in so that the trespass might increase (see Romans 7:7-12) but where sin increased, grace increased all the more, so that, just as sin reigned in death, so also grace might reign through righteousness to bring eternal life through Jesus Christ our Lord'.

Part 3

The World

Maurice Buckmaster was the head of the French section of the Special Operations Executive (SOE), and under his leadership agents were sent into France to coordinate resistance and information gathering against the occupying German forces.

Each agent was taught to use security codes and special signals in their radio messages. All had their own coding system, transmission times and frequencies. In the eventuality that they were captured they had two security checks, one was a bluff check and the other, a true check. They also had different ways of signing off. The purpose of the bluff check was that if they were tortured they would give the bluff check only and London would then know that the Germans had them.

Buckmaster was informed by operators receiving the agents messages that they had serious concerns that some of them were not including their second checks, and that there were other irregularities, this, Buckmaster put down to forgetfulness or carelessness due to difficult conditions.

He was very reluctant to accept that some of his agents were in German hands. Dick White, an assistant director of MI5 in March 1943, wrote, 'Perhaps the most important (example) of all is that of the SOE organisation in Belgium which ran for many months without SOE realising that it was almost completely under the control of the Germans'. There was little contact between those running operations in the various European sections for fear of leaks even though they shared the same building and relations with MI5 and M16 were not good, as well as General Charles de Gaulle having set up his government-in-exile in London in June 1940, who established his own secret service department and considered that the SOE were infringing the sovereignty of France, which made relations between SOE and the Free French extremely difficult.

Buckmaster's response to these questionable messages was to signal back 'You have forgotten your double security check, be more careful next time'. The Germans who received this message realised that the captured agent had been concealing the fact that he had a second security check. The absence of the check in his message should have warned London that he was caught. Needless to say, one agent was shocked and angry when a German officer told him how much they knew, and that London could be capable of such terrible incompetence.

A few of the SOE team knew that the signals from the agents were phoney but were unable to convince Buckmaster to end the contact. This happened repeatedly, and warnings by his own staff were ignored. Vera Atkins (formally Rosenberg) who was the intelligence officer for F section and close to Buckmaster, needed him to back her request for naturalisation, because she was originally from Romania and was Jewish, and although she had strong doubts about some of the agents' messages she did not challenge him on it, so a chance to correct this great error was missed.

Buckmaster had also personally recruited a French airman, Henri Déricourt, who became F section's new air movements officer. He was to organise the night landings and pick-up operations. He was parachuted back to France and air operations in and out of France ran more smoothly than before.

His charms had not only impressed Buckmaster and most of F section but also the Lysander pilots known as the 'Moon Squadron'. He was also the 'postman' responsible for collecting the agent's letters and putting them on the planes. He did his job very well and there was only one problem, he was working for the Germans. A total of fifty-four agents who landed in France passed through his hands and twenty-seven SOE agents were captured on landing or very soon afterwards, most of which were shot or hanged including the women agents, four of whom, Andree Borrel, Vera Leigh, Sonia Olschanesky and Diana Rowden died in Natzweiler concentration camp in horrific circumstances.

Henri Déricourt was not only a traitor but also a brilliant conman. Many years after the war Buckmaster attended a ceremony in memory of one of the British agents, Nora Inayat Khan who was beaten to death in Dachau. Nora's elder brother, Vilayat clearly remembered how Buckmaster had broken down in tears at the ceremony, he had bitterly regretted sending Nora and was overcome with remorse and said that he could never forgive himself. *From Sarah Helm's 'A life in Secrets'*

The message that was given to the church has, in part, fallen into the enemies hands. He too is a brilliant con-being and has, through human hands, distorted the good news of the Kingdom of God into something else – an eternity in heaven. It's what most Christians believe yet it's not what Jesus or the apostles taught. The leaders of SOE were warned that something was wrong, but they ignored it. There is something wrong in the churches' message and sadly most will ignore any warnings, just as Buckmaster did. It was said that Buckmaster was 'full of understandable optimism and a natural unwillingness to regard an agent as lost, particularly if he liked or had befriended them'.

Perhaps the most well-known verse in the bible is John 3:16: 'For God so loved the world that he gave his one and only Son, that whoever believes in him shall not perish but have eternal life'. God's will is not that people perish, but that they are saved from destruction. The prophet Ezekiel wrote that God does not take any pleasure in the death of the wicked, but is pleased when they turn from their ways and live. God's message through Ezekiel was that we should repent (a radical change of mind and heart) and live, Ezek 18:23,32.

Peter was inspired to write, 'the Lord is not slow in keeping his promise, as some understand slowness. He is patient with you, not wanting anyone to perish, but everyone to come to repentance' 2 Peter 3:9. It is through God's kindness that we are led towards repentance Rom 2:4. Paul writes to Timothy saying, 'Opponents must be gently instructed, in the hope that God will grant them repentance leading them to a knowledge of the truth, and that they will come to their senses and escape from the trap of the devil, who has taken them captive to do his will' 2 Tim 2:25-26.

The Dragon has led astray and deceived the whole world, Rev 12:9.

This clear biblical statement reveals the spiritual condition of world-wide deception that exists for all mankind. Revelation 13 goes into great detail in highly symbolic language how this deception works from the top down and in so doing governs the lives of millions of people. At some future time, the dragon will give the beast, who John 'saw' coming out of the sea, representing a powerful tyranny. This beast resembles the forth beast of Daniel, chapter 7. Then John saw another beast that looked like a lamb, but it spoke like a dragon. This beast used its authority to lead the world in worshipping the first beast and it was able to deceive all because of incredible signs it was able to do. It will only last for the same time period we read about in chapter 12 – forty-two months – if that is how we should understand it. Prophecy is best understood in hindsight.

Paul wrote to the Thessalonians that the 'coming of the lawless one will be in accordance with the works of Satan displayed in all kinds of counterfeit miracles, signs and wonders, and in every sort of evil that deceives those who are perishing. They perish because they refused to love the truth and so be saved. For this reason God sends them a powerful delusion so that they will believe the lie and so that all will be condemned who have not believed the truth but have delighted in wickedness' 2 Thes 2:9-12.

Those lies will appear as truth, just as today many claim to represent what is true and have convinced many to believe what they say. Some of those major untruths will be delt with in the following chapters.

The people who aggressively resisted Jesus the most were the ones we might think would be the most positive and welcoming – the religious leaders – those who Paul said had the advantage of being entrusted with the very word of God, Rom 3:1-2.

Paul was able to describe them so well because he used to be one of them. He reminded the Galatians how he was advancing in Judaism beyond many of the Jews of his own age and was extremely zealous for the traditions of his fathers, Gal1:14. Like the other Pharisees, he relied on the law, much of which was added after they had returned from deportation centuries before, and bragged about his relationship with God, thinking he knew God's will and approved of what is superior because of being instructed by the law. He was convinced that he was a guide for the blind, a light for those in the dark, that he was an instructor of the foolish, a teacher of infants, because he had in the law the embodiment of knowledge and truth, Rom 2:17-20.

This was all very impressive and the religious leaders did little to dissuade the people from that view. They had the knowledge and capabilities that most people did not have, and in their position of authority what person could, or would, challenge them? Who would dare say to them that their understanding was faulty and to condemn them as overly critical, hair splitting, pedantic, and legalistic religious types? They were openly demonstrating that their father was not God but the dragon.

Jesus told them these unwelcome truths and did not soften his words to spare their sensitive feelings. He did not have a message of God's love for them but spoke to them as enemies of God, 'Woe to you, teachers of the law and Pharisees, you hypocrites. You shut the kingdom of heaven (Matthew limits his use of the word 'God') in men's faces. You yourselves do not enter, nor will you let those enter who are trying to' Matt 23:13. They had carefully cultivated an image of piety that had to be maintained. They played their religious role with an eye to being noticed – whether it was praying or giving or fasting – it was done to be seen.

Mark, in his gospel, presents this conflict in the account of the healing of a man with a shrivelled hand. It happened on the Sabbath and some of those in the synagogue were looking for a reason to accuse Jesus, so they watched him closely to see if he would heal the man on the day of rest. Jesus, knowing what their attitude was, said to the man with the damaged hand, 'Stand up in front of everyone'. Then Jesus asked his critics, 'Which is lawful on the Sabbath: to do good or to do evil, to save life or to kill?' but they remained silent.

He looked round at them in anger and deeply distressed at their stubborn hearts, said to the man, 'Stretch out your hand'. He stretched it out and his hand was completely restored. Then the Pharisees went out and began to plot with the Herodians how they might kill Jesus, Mark 3:1-6.

It was because of their hard-hearted attitude to how to observe the Sabbath that aroused their hatred of Jesus as someone who, in their eyes, was desecrating a sacred day. Their God was only interested in how well they kept the law and they knew nothing of the love of God.

Jesus knew that this hostile response to what he said and did happened because they were listening, not to God, but to the dragon, who was close to them.

Jesus said to his violent critics, 'I know that you are Abraham's descendants, yet you are ready to kill me because you have no room for my word – I am telling you what I have seen in the Father's presence, and you do what you have heard from your father'. 'Abraham is our father', they answered. 'If you were Abraham's children', said Jesus, 'then you would do what Abraham did. As it is, you are looking for a way to kill me, a man who has told you the truth that I heard from God. Abraham did not do such things. You are doing the works of your own father'. 'We are not illegitimate children', they protested. 'The only Father we have is God himself'. Jesus said to them, 'If God were your Father, you would love me, for I came from God and now am here. I have not come on my own; but he sent me. Why is my language not clear to you? Because you are unable to hear what I say. You belong to your father, the devil, and you want to carry out your father's desires. He was a murderer from the beginning, not holding to the truth, for there is no truth in him. When he lies, he speaks his native language, for he is a liar and the father of lies. Yet because I tell you the truth, you do not believe me. Can any of you prove me guilty of sin? If I am telling you the truth, why don't you believe me? Whoever belongs to God hears what God says. The reason you do not hear is that you do not belong to God' John 8:37-47.

The dragon's real and dark influence runs wider and deeper than any of us have imagined. He works through deception and is so effective that people professing Christianity can confidently say they are serving God when they are in fact acting out the will of the unseen ruler and prince of this world. 'We know', John wrote, 'that we are the children of God, and that the whole world is under the control of the evil one' 1 John 5:19.

Jesus told his disciples, 'All this I have told you so that you will not go astray. They will put you out of the synagogue; in fact, a time is coming when anyone who kills you will think he is offering a service to God' John 16: 1-2.

Just before saying this Jesus had told them that, 'if the world hates you, keep in mind that it hated me first. If you belonged to the world, it would love you as its own. As it is, you do not belong to the world, but I have chosen you out of the world. That is why the world hates you' John 15:18-19.

When, on that last night, Jesus prayed to his Father for his disciples, he said, 'I have revealed you to those whom you gave me out of the world ... I pray for them. I am not praying for the world, but for those you have given me, for they are yours ... I have given them your word and the world has hated them, for they are not of the world. My prayer is not that you take them out of the world but that you protect them from the evil one.

'They are not of the world, even as I am not of it. Sanctify them by the truth; your word is truth. As you sent me into the world, I have sent them into the world' John 17:6-18.

This world is enemy territory and there is a real spiritual war that most people are unaware of. When most of Western Europe was under the control of Nazism, the populations of those nations had to wait while they suffered under that cruel power until their liberation came and they were released from that tyranny. Unknown to the world's populations an evil force is in occupation; they are the powers of this dark world and the spiritual forces of evil in the heavenly realms Eph 6:12.

They will not be removed until Christ returns. All systems, political, religious and social, have been influenced, more than we have realised, by the being that Jesus called the prince of this world,

John 12:31, 14:30, 16:11. Jesus used the word 'now' twice in John 12:31 so it appears that both Jesus and John the Baptist and the apostles, in what they said and wrote, expected the second coming to be very soon – in their lifetime, but God has delayed the second coming for his own purposes. It is still in the future.

Jesus personally experienced the temptations of the dragon who suggested in different ways that Jesus had the option of an easier, quicker and more pleasant way to achieve his goals. In one of the temptations the dragon took Jesus to a very high mountain and displayed all the kingdoms of the world and their splendour, and he said to Jesus, 'All this I will give you, for it has been given to me, and I can give it to anyone I want to. So if you worship me, it will all be yours'. Jesus responded with what is the essence of a Christian's life, 'Worship the Lord your God and serve him only'. He is the only one who has perfectly done this.

Jesus rejected taking over the world on the dragon's terms because his kingdom is not of this world. His kingdom comes from heaven and comes with his return and cannot be established by any church or combination of churches in this age, which is under the control of the dragon.

All the good work that Christian individuals

and groups do around the world and in your neighbourhood will not bring peace – even Jesus said that he did not come to bring peace, Luke 12:51. It will take something far greater than Christians to transform this world. It will only be accomplished by the return of the King, who proved himself fully obedient, unlike Adam, whom we have all followed.

Years later Paul wrote, 'I consider that our present sufferings are not worth comparing with the glory that will be revealed in us. The creation waits in eager expectation for the sons of God to be revealed. For the creation was subjected to frustration, not by its own choice, but by the will of the one who subjected it, in hope that the creation itself will be liberated from its bondage to decay and brought into the glorious freedom of the children of God', Rom 8: 18-21.

Jesus sent his disciples into the world as sheep among wolves; they were to be as shrewd as snakes and as innocent as doves. They were to be lights in a darkened world and ambassadors of Christ with his message of reconciliation, 2 Cor 5: 18-20.

The writer of Hebrews spoke of the people of faith who were given promises yet died not having received them; 'they only saw them and welcomed them from a distance. And they admitted that they were aliens and strangers on earth. People who say such things show that they are looking for a country of their own … they are longing for a better country – a heavenly one. Therefore God is not ashamed to be called their God, for he has prepared a city for them' Heb 11: 13-16.

The subject of heaven is one that needs to be revisited as the dragon has misrepresented what the Bible teaches concerning this important issue.

Part 4

Heaven

Many people, even though they may disagree on doctrinal points, draw great comfort from the belief that a loved one who has died has gone directly to be with Jesus and is now in glory. For those who do not have any strong beliefs there is still a conviction that a good person will be in a better place – wherever and whatever that place is. We express what happens when we die in many different ways: we pass on, we go to heaven, we're with the Lord in glory, we're amongst the stars, we become stardust, we return to dust, we're going home, we're reincarnated. And many who honestly admit that they have no idea.

It is commonly believed that we all have an immortal soul and if that is true then the soul does have to go somewhere when we die, or as I read on a piece of evangelical literature, 'man is an eternal being'. This has been, and remains, a fundamental understanding that at death our soul enters a new and different spiritual experience that many cultures are convinced of and some call it heaven.

This belief in the soul's immortality goes back to the earliest civilisations but it was Plato (428-347 B.C.) Who taught that only a transcendent realm of 'Ideas' or 'forms' was permanent and true, and was the ultimate reality. Humans, he taught, were composed of two parts, a limited human body and an immortal soul, and the soul's origins were in the world of Ideas. This soul was imprisoned in the body and pre-existed in that greater reality of the ultimate ideal, known as the principal of the Good.

After Plato's death, Platonism went through a series of phases, each with its own distinctive emphases and styles, and in time it would exercise a very strong influence over Christian thinking. Stoicism and Epicureanism also had a wide-reaching effect on early church leaders. These philosophies nourished the culture and thinking of many of the early church fathers who blended what was considered the best of worldly wisdom with the scriptures, and was often the starting point of their education even before they came to the scriptures.

It was thought that philosophy was able to teach people much about the nature of God. As the law was to the Hebrews; in charge to lead them to Christ, Gal 3:24, so philosophy was to the Greeks; a tutor to bring them to Christ. The teaching of those considered to be the wise of the world was seen as an important preparation for the gospel, without it people were considered as uneducated.

This has a significant connection with what is generally assumed and taught within Christianity: that our soul is immortal. Yet, and it's a big yet, it is completely absent from both the Old and New Testaments. The word soul, as used in the King James Version, is just an old-fashioned way of saying, a person. A good example of this Ezekiel 18:4, which in a contemporary version reads '… The one who sins is the one who will die'. While in the AV we read, 'the soul that sinneth, it shall die'. The soul is another way of speaking of a human being, physical and mortal. Peter Lewis, in his book 'The Glory of Christ' writes, 'It is true that the idea that the soul is immortal by nature, that immortality is an innate quality of the human soul, is a Greek idea and not a biblical. However, we can claim the idea of the immortality of the soul as a biblical one, and not merely a philosophical idea, if we are clear that immortality is a gift of *creation* (not simply of redemption), and is bound up with God's intention of what human beings should be. Hence when God says, 'Let us make man in our image, after our likeness' he is announcing a decision to share his own everlasting existence with men and women.

Immortality, then, is intrinsic to what it is to be human in God's sight, and it is a gift'.

On the one hand he can say that immortality is a Greek idea, and on the other hand say that we can claim the idea of the immortality of the soul as a biblical one. Clever reasoning, as this is, can lead many to accept pagan philosophies as biblical.

John Calvin's first theological book '*De Psycopannychia*' (On the sleep of the soul) 1534, was aiming at a false target for the Bible never speaks of the soul sleeping; soul sleep is not a biblical expression. The term Paul used was asleep or sleeping (1Cor 11:30, 15:6, 18, 20, 51. 1Thes 4:13-15). Luke writes, 'he fell asleep' in writing of Stephen's death, Acts 7:60. David writes that the dead neither remembers or praises God in the grave Psa 6:5, and in Psalm 13:3, he writes, 'I will sleep in death'.

While east of the Jordan, after leaving Jerusalem, Jesus told his disciples that they would return to Judea and visit Lazurus who was unwell. 'Our friend Lazurus has fallen asleep; but I am going there to wake him up'. 'Lord, if he sleeps, he will get better,' his disciples replied. Jesus had been speaking of his death, but his disciples thought he meant natural sleep. So then he told them plainly, 'Lazurus is dead'.

Jesus used, as others did, the metaphor of sleep in talking of death with the implication that at some time you will wake up. Because in God's eyes no one is truly dead. In replying to the Sadducees, who did not believe that there would be a resurrection, Jesus said to them, 'You are in error because you do not know the scriptures or the power of God. At the resurrection people will neither marry nor be given in marriage; they will be like the angels in heaven. But about the resurrection of the dead – have you not read what God said to you, 'I am the God of Abraham, the God of Isaac, and the God of Jacob'? He is not the God of the dead but of the living'.

Later, Jesus said, 'Very truly I tell you, whoever hears my word and believes him who sent me has eternal life and will not be judged but has crossed over from death to life. A time is coming and has now come when the dead will hear the voice of the Son of God and those who hear will live. For as the Father has life in himself, so he has granted the Son also to have life in himself. And he has given him authority to judge because he is the Son of Man.

'Do not be amazed at this, for a time is coming when all who are in their graves will hear his voice and come out – those who have done what is good will rise to live, and those who have done what is evil will rise to be condemned' John 5:24-29.

Paul wrote to the Thessalonians about believers who had died: 'Brothers and sisters, we do not want you to be uninformed about those who sleep in death, so you do not grieve like the rest, who have no hope. We believe that Jesus died and rose again, and so we believe that God will bring with Jesus those who have fallen asleep in him. According to the Lord's word, we tell you that we who are still alive, who are left till the coming of the Lord, will certainly not precede those who have fallen asleep. For the Lord himself will come down from heaven, with a loud command, with the voice of the archangel and with the trumpet call of God, and the dead in Christ will rise first. After that, we who are still alive and are left will be caught up together with them in the clouds to meet the Lord in the air. And so we will be with the Lord for ever. Therefore encourage one another with these words' 1Thes 4:13-18.

We need, at this point, to speak about the 'Rapture' which many people, in reading the previous text, understand it as saying that when Jesus returns he is only descending to the clouds, collecting his people and then returning to heaven. To do what and for how long, and why? These are questions that are not answered. So Jesus would then, sometime later return which would make that his third coming. Nowhere in scripture does it imply that Jesus does a U-turn when he returns but rather continues to descend while destroying those who oppose him and touching down on the Mount of olives as described in Zechariah 14:14.

'Just as people are destined to die once, and after that to face judgment, so Christ was sacrificed once to take away the sins of many; and he will appear a second time, not to bear sin, but to bring salvation to those who are waiting for him' Hebrews 9:27.

Many might say, 'didn't Jesus say, 'great is your reward in heaven'. Yes he did, but that doesn't mean you're going there to receive it, rather, Jesus is bringing it with him. See Isaiah 40:10, 62:11and Rev 22:12.

Some might point to the promise that Jesus gave to the repentant criminal on the cross, 'I tell you the truth, today you will be with me in paradise' Luke 23:43. Jesus was not in paradise that day as he remained dead for three days and three nights and after his resurrection he told Mary Magdalene that he had not yet ascended, 'to my Father and your Father, to my God and your God', so how are we to understand that statement in Luke?

Originally the words spoken on the cross were in Aramaic, then written in Greek, then written in

English. Of course, in the Greek there are no full stops or commas so they had to be placed where it was considered appropriate. The late biblical scholar, Leon Morris, writes in his commentary on Luke 23:43, '*Today* is occasionally taken with the preceding words, but there seems no reason for this.' One good reason for putting the comma after *today* would mean that Jesus told the man that 'he would be in paradise', but not until the resurrection.

Was not Elijah taken up into heaven in a whirlwind? Yes, but the sky is also called heaven in the Bible. He was moved to another location some distance away and later wrote a letter to king Jehoram, 2 Chronicles 21:12.

There are only two types of bodies: our physical bodies and the glorious and powerful spiritual bodies that are given at the resurrection, so if there are people in heaven now, what bodies do they have?

A young man was being interviewed on TBN UK about how real and exciting the prospect of going to heaven became for him when he read in Paul's letter to the Corinthians that when he got to heaven his body would be imperishable, glorious, powerful and spiritual. This, for him, made the belief in going to heaven much more thrilling than he had felt before. Sadly, heaven is not the subject in that section of the text. He was quoting from 1Cor 15:42-44. The section begins in verse 35, 'But someone will ask, 'How are the dead raised? With what kind of body will they come?''. The whole chapter deals with the resurrection, not going to heaven. He, and many others, have been misled while the Bible is clear in teaching that we are mortal and sleep in death until the resurrection – either the first, to immortality or the second, to judgment.

Why does the dragon want to deceive people about their ultimate destination? He deliberately misdirects people just as a person who wilfully misdirects a child is rightly condemned – the dragon is condemned because he is a liar, and misdirects people.

Heaven is a wonderful place of incredible colour, sound and majesty, filled with heavenly creatures and holiness. Why would the dragon be pleased if all believed that heaven was the place they were going to? Because if our focus is on the greatness and splendour of eternal life in heaven then we would have been redirected away from the future of this world and the work that God is preparing us for.

December 7. 1941. Singapore.

The managing director and editor of the Malaya Tribune, Jimmy Glover, was afraid of the future. The Sunday edition of his newspaper had the ominous headline, **27 JAPANESE TRANSPORTS SIGHTED OFF CAMBODIA POINT.** These ships were, according to the details that followed, steaming west towards the east coast of Malaya or southern Siam.

This event was too big to be suppressed and there was already an official announcement telling people not to travel, and urging those on holiday to return home. Glover wondered how long the peace and serenity of Singapore would last.

He received a telephone call from Air Chief Marshall Sir Robert Brooke-Popham, Commander-in-Chief of the Far East, in person, and very angry. He was complaining about the Tribune's 'pessimistic view of the Far East situation.'

'I consider it most improper to print such alarmist views at a time like the present, the position isn't half so serious as the Tribune makes out.'

'That's not fair', Glover replied, 'the news was released by Reuter's and passed by the censor. To me, the presence of those Japanese transports off Cambodia Point means war.'

December 26.

The situation had dramatically deteriorated, the Japanese never slowed down and time after time the British, Australian or Indian troops were annihilated by skilful Japanese enveloping tactics. On the British side wrong decisions were made. Communications broke down. Orders went astray. Whole pockets of troops were cut off. The first Japanese tanks appeared and 'came as a great surprise' to the British who had not one single tank in Malaya.

It was at this time that an extraordinary secret meeting took place between General Percival, the Commanding Officer, and Brigadier Ivan Simson, his chief Engineer.

Simson's attempts to improve and add to the defences had been blocked at every turn, largely by General Percival, who seemed to have a fixation against such measures. Above everything else, Simson was most concerned about the complete lack of defences on the north shores of Singapore Island, facing Johore, and now becoming increasingly vital as the Japanese advanced southwards. Nothing had been done, nothing was to be done, despite many previous pleas.

Simson had felt for a long time that his only

chance of ever persuading Percival to throw up any defences on the north shores lay in getting the General alone. That opportunity arrived – at 11.30 p.m. on Boxing Day.

Percival was just about to go to bed and looked with some astonishment at this late visitor. When Simson announced that he carried an important message given him by General Heath, Percival invited him in. The Brigadier gave Percival the message – and instead of leaving, said that he needed to speak about the defences. Percival looked 'a trifle startled' but sat down with a tired expression and listened.

Simson said he had the staff and materials to throw up fixed and semi-permanent defences, anti-tank defences, under-water obstacles, fire traps, mines, anchored but floating barbed wire, methods of illuminating the water at night. And since it now seemed inevitable that the Japanese would soon reach Johore and attack the Island across the narrow straits, the matter was one of extreme urgency. But it could be done, said Simson.

To the Brigadier's dismay. Percival refused his request, but Simson said, 'Sir, I must emphasise the urgency of doing everything to help our troops, they're often only partially trained, they're tired and dispirited, they've been retreating for hundreds of miles, and please remember, sir, the Japanese are better trained, better equipped, and they're inspired by an unbroken run of victories.'

As the clock moved round to one in the morning and he seemed to be making no impression, Simson found it hard to control his anger.

'And it has to be done now, sir, once the area comes under fire, civilian labour will vanish. But if we start now we can do it.'

Incredibly, Percival still refused to change his mind.

'Look here, General – I've raised this question time after time, you've always refused, what's more, you've always refused to give me any reasons, at least tell me one thing – why on earth are you taking this stand?'

It was at this point that Percival finally gave his answer. 'I believe that defences of the sort you want to throw up are bad for the morale of troops and civilians.'

Simson was 'frankly horrified' and remembers standing there in the room, suddenly feeling quite cold, and realising that, except for a miracle, Singapore was as good as lost.

Simson make one last remark, 'Sir, it's going

to be much worse for morale if the Japanese start running all over the Island.'

It was just two o' clock on the morning of December 27.

At 6.10p.m. February15, General Percival signed the surrender of Singapore in the presence of General Tomoyuki Yamashita, Commander-in-Chief of all Japanese forces in Malaya. A hundred thousand British and Imperial troops became prisoners of war.

From Noel Barber's 'Sinister Twilight'

Part 5

Restoration

You might have noticed that when people speak about going to heaven little is said regarding what is going to happen to earth. Some believe it will be left a smoking ruin inhabited by demons, others might say that after a thousand years in heaven they will return to earth to await the heavenly city to descend. For many the good news is life in heaven and what happens on earth holds little interest for them.

The Father sent his Son to be the Saviour of the world, 1 John 4:14, not to destroy it. Jesus is not returning to earth to pick up his people and do a U-turn back to heaven. He is the returning King, he is the 'man of noble birth who went to a distant country to have himself appointed king and then to return' Luke 19:12. One of the first things that will be done on his return is the seizure of the dragon so that he will not be able to deceive the nations for a thousand years, Rev 20:1-3. This is not what the dragon wants you to look forward to. Liberation is not solely the rescuing of people but the effective ending of the enemy's rule.

The prophets of the Old Testament were given many inspiring visions of an earth that enters a new age, an age where a divine government will bring peace to earth, not the peace on earth that is read and sang over the Christmas period, which presents a false message of why Jesus came, but real peace that will cover the whole world.

Dale Ralph Davis has written helpful commentaries on the historical books of the Bible, from Joshua to 2 Kings. He has also written on Psalms 1-12 in a book titled 'The Way of the Righteous in the Muck of Life.' In writing on Psalm 2 he says, 'the position of these two psalms (1&2) at the beginning of the Psalter is deliberate. Psalm 1 deals with the most urgent individual matter; you must know where you are going and must be sure you belong to the congregation of the righteous. Psalm 2 says you must know where history is going; you must see the whole show; you must understand that *the world has been promised to the Messiah.*'

'... Here is a hostile world – nations rage, peoples plot, kings and rulers conspire against Yahweh and his anointed King. Whether congress or parliaments, whether democracies or dictatorships, the root attitude of nations and of the head knockers of this age is: 'We do not want this man to rule over us' Luke 19:14. This is Psalm 1:1 to the second power and writ large; this is what it looks like when the council of the wicked and the way of sinners and the seat of scoffers goes international.'

Davis comments on the decree of the Lord, 7-9. 'There are three keynotes in this decree about the Messiah's reign. The first is *legitimacy*: 'You are my son; I have begotten you this very day' 7b. Yahweh has appointed him to rule and has installed him. He is the rightful king. Then there is the *scope* of his rule in verse 8 'nations ... ends of the earth' – his will be an international, world-wide kingdom. It is all to belong to Jesus. And then he indicates the *force* of his rule in verse 9: 'You will break them with an iron rod, you will smash them to pieces like a clay pot.

'Why, we might think, I was just beginning to warm to Christ's kingdom and then, suddenly, it turns vicious. But you must understand verse 9 in the light of verse 3. When the time comes to fully enforce his kingly rule, Christ will not be welcomed with open arms. He comes to a God-hating, Christ-defying world. The kingdom of our Lord and of his Christ imposes his reign by force on rebellious people. So get the picture the decree gives you: The appointed King, v.7 with world-wide sway, v.8 to be established in overwhelming force, v.9. That is the decree that is controlling history.'

After the violent takeover of the world's governments 'Many nations will come and say, 'Come, let us go up to the mountain of the Lord, to the house of the God of Jacob. He will teach us his ways, so that we may walk in his paths.' The law will go out from Zion, the word of the Lord from Jerusalem. He will judge between many peoples and will settle disputes for strong nations far and wide. They will beat their swords into ploughshares and their spears into pruning hooks. Nation will not take up sword against nation, nor will they train for war any more. Every man will sit under his own vine and under his own fig-tree, and no-one will make them afraid, for the Lord Almighty has spoken' Micah 4: 2-4.

The dragon wants to take our focus away from the kingdom of God on earth to eternal life in heaven and all the pleasures and joys that will be there. In this he has been successful. The shift towards the teaching of going to heaven began early in church history.

'Irenaeus, 140-200, saw the kingdom of God as very much a physical phenomenon, and he taught the prospect of an earthly reign of God as part of the eschatological vision for creation. His millenarianism, based on a fairly literal reading of the vision in Revelation 20:1-6 of a future thousand-year reign of God on earth, would in time render his writings less influential in the East than they proved to be in the West, as Greek theology on the whole came to be less enamoured of such a literal interpretation of Revelation's language. There were, however, strong millennial views among many Gnostics and Montanists, and also in writers such as Justin Martyr.' 'The Birth of the Church' Ivor J. Davidson, pp. 227, 383, note 3.

Edward Gibbon writes in chapter 15 of his 'Decline and fall of the Roman Empire' 'The ancient and popular doctrine of the Millennium was intimately connected with the second coming of Christ. As the works of the creation had been finished in six days, their duration in their present state ...was fixed to six thousand years. By the same analogy it was inferred that this long period of labour and contention, which was now almost elapsed, would be succeeded by a joyful Sabbath of a thousand years; and that Christ, with the triumphant band of the saints and the elect who had escaped death, or who had been miraculously revived, would reign upon earth till the time appointed for the last and general resurrection ... The doctrine of Christ's reign upon earth was at first treated as a profound allegory, was considered by degrees as a doubtful and useless opinion, and was at length rejected as the absurd invention of heresy and fanaticism'. The writer of the letter to the Hebrews talks about the Israelites who because of their hard hearts did not enter 'my rest' the promised land, but died in the desert, and he goes on the say, 'Today, if you hear his voice do not harden your hearts (quoting Psalm 95), for if Joshua had given them rest, God would not have spoken later about another day. There remains then, a Sabbath-rest for the people of God.' There has been four-thousand years of human history before the time of Christ, and two-thousand years since that time. We are now close to the end of that six-thousand-year period, and perhaps, approaching to that thousand year 'rest'.

Those early groups, like today, had some serious misunderstandings over doctrine, but it does not mean that they were wrong in everything they taught. Yet there is no one denomination that has not been touched, to one degree or another, by the dragon's deceptions. Each fellowship is careful and dedicated to preserve and protect what they consider as biblical truth while condemning what they consider as heresy from other fellowships yet, all too often, they appear blind to their own errors.

Part 6

Hell

If we misunderstood the biblical teaching about heaven, could we also have got our thinking about hell wrong as well?

Many reluctantly, and some, enthusiastically, believe in eternal torment for the wicked because they are convinced that the bible teaches that it is deserved. It seems to have been taught throughout church history and paintings and frescos have attempted to make it real and shocking, as well as a basic biblical teaching.

The late Iain M. Banks, the sci-fi writer, had this traditional view of hell in his mind when he was writing 'Surface Detail'. Here's a sample, 'There were many thousands of such unfortunates to be bled during each session and they were duly dragged screaming from their nearby pens by grotesquely formed, irresistibly powerful demons and strapped to canted iron tables with drains at their foot ... Some were told the mill did power something. They were told it held great stone wheels which ground the bodies and bones of those guilty of crimes committed within hell. Those so punished suffered even greater agonies than those bodies still in some sense resembled those they inhabited before death; for those who had sinned even within Hell, the rules – always entirely flexible – were changed so that they could suffer with every sinew, cell and structure of their body, no matter how atomised it might have become and how impossible such suffering would have been with an utterly shredded nervous central system in the Real' pp.45,47.

Now, we'll move from fiction to fact. Samuel Davis, 1723-1761, was a Presbyterian preacher in America who was part of the religious revival known as the Great Awakening. This is what he wrote for a sermon called 'The General Resurrection', 'The bodies of the wicked will also be improved, but their improvements will all be terrible and vindictive. Their capacities will be thoroughly enlarged, but then it will be that they may be made capable of greater misery. They will be strengthened, but it will be that they may bear the heavier load of torment. Their sensations will be more quick and strong, but it will be that they may feel the more exquisite pain. They will be raised immortal that they may not be consumed by everlasting fire or escape punishment by destruction or annihilation. In short, their augmented strength, their enlarged capacities, and their immortality will be their eternal curse. They would willingly exchange them for fleeting duration of a fading flower or the faint sensations of an infant. The only power they would rejoice in is that of self-annihilation.'

Whether it is from the writer of fiction or a minister of the church, the teaching of hell is horrific. What is worse is that this doctrine is not biblical, and think for a moment of all those millions of people that have been misled by this dragon inspired teaching.

A well-known contemporary evangelist suggests that we must take the time to educate an unbelieving person in the theology of hell with these words, 'Do you know what hell is like? There is weeping and gnashing of teeth, unending thirst, mind-consuming pain, no ground or foundation – the sensation of always falling. Very hot, and it lasts forever.'

Another evangelist, who has an established international reputation, writes, 'First, hell is a place of constant torment, misery and pain. The torment is often described as darkness, Matt 22:13, where no light can penetrate, and nothing can be seen. Throughout the numberless eons of eternity the damned will never again see light or anything that light illumines. Hell's torment is also described as fire that will never go out and cannot be extinguished, Mark 9:43, and from which the damned will never find relief. Hell could not be other than a place where there shall be weeping and gnashing of teeth.

Missionaries have travelled to remote areas of the world to teach people that their immortal souls would not go to heaven but will suffer in hell for an eternity if their didn't accept their version of the good news.

Jesus called his people 'a little flock' and he warned his disciples that 'many will come in his name claiming the he (Jesus) is the Christ (the Messiah or Anointed One) and will deceive many'.

One of the main texts used by those who pass on this message of eternal suffering is Mark 9: 48, 'their worm does not die, and the fire is not quenched.' He had just said, 'It is better for you to enter the kingdom of God with one eye than to have two eyes and be thrown into hell, where …'

Just one more paragraph from this well-known writer, 'Jesus spoke of hell as a place *where their worm does not die*. When physical bodies are buried and begin to decay, the worms can attack them only as long as the flesh lasts. Once consumed, the body can experience no more harm. But the resurrected bodies of unbelievers will never be consumed, and the hellish 'worms' that feed on them will themselves never die.'

Jesus was quoting from the last verse in the book of Isaiah, so it would be helpful if we read what Jesus quoted from: 'And they will go out and look on the dead bodies of those who rebelled against me; their worm will not die, nor will their fire be quenched, and they will be loathsome to the whole human race.' A dreadful picture, but these maggot-infested bodies of those who rebelled against God are all dead.

There was, in the time of Jesus, a site, just outside of Jerusalem, which was used as a public rubbish tip where carcases, both animal and human could be burnt because that area was considered desecrated ground fit only to burn refuse. The place was the valley of Hinnom and it is where the word Gehenna comes from and is the word Jesus used. Hell was not a word he would have known as it comes from 'Hel', the old Norse goddess of the dead. This valley of Hinnom was used hundreds of years before as a place for child sacrifice to the gods that were worshipped then. Jeremiah writes of what was done there in chapter 19:1-6.

Jesus said to his disciples, 'things that cause people to sin are bound to come, but woe to that person through whom they come. It would be better for him to be thrown into the sea with a millstone tied round his neck than for him to cause one of these little ones to sin. So watch yourselves ...' Luke 17:1-3.

To die that way, in the sea, is a terrible way to go, and yet, Jesus said it would be better to die that way than face the consequences of causing a person to sin. What would those consequences be? Paul wrote that the wages of sin is death, Rom 6:23. The fate of the wicked is to be burned to ashes. John the Baptist pictured it as 'burning up the chaff' Matt 3:12, while Malachi puts it this way, 'Surely the day is coming; it will burn like a furnace. All the arrogant and every evildoer will be stubble, and that day that is coming will set them on fire ... not a root or a branch will be left to them ... they will be ashes under the soles of your feet' Mal 4:1-3.

Jesus used the analogy of gathering in the harvest when he said, in the parable of the weeds, 'Let both grow together until the harvest. At that time I will tell the harvesters: first collect the weeds and tie them in bundles to be burned; then gather the wheat and bring it into my barn' Matt 13:30.

Peter gives us an example from biblical history.

'He condemned the cities of Sodom and Gomorrah by burning them to ashes, and made them an example of what is going to happen to the ungodly' 2 Peter 2:6.

In verse 4 of Peter's second letter, chapter 2, we read, 'For if God did not spare angels when they sinned but sent them to hell, putting them in chains of darkness to be held for judgment …' The word hell mentioned in this verse is not *Gehenna*, the word Jesus used when he spoke of the fate of the unrepentant wicked but *Tartarus*, a Greek word signifying the spiritual imprisonment of those fallen angels between the time of Adam and Noah who, as Genesis 6:2 tells us, 'the sons of God saw that these daughters were beautiful, and they married any of them they chose'. These created beings were fallen angels who belonged to the dragon. Verse 4 of Genesis 2 has, 'The Nephilim were on the earth in those days – and also afterwards – when the sons of God went to the daughters of the human beings and had children by them. They were the heroes of old, men of renown'. Nephilim means 'Fallen Ones'. Jude1:6 adds to the picture, 'And the angels who did not keep their positions of authority but abandoned their proper dwelling – these he has kept in darkness, bound with everlasting chains for Judgment on the great Day'.

When Jesus was resurrected, at sunset on the weekly Sabbath, (there were two Sabbaths that week – the first of the annual Sabbaths plus the weekly Sabbath. Mark 16:9 has, *'When Jesus rose early on the first day of the week...'* most translations have a note saying that verses 9-20 were added later, when Sunday replaced Saturday as the day of rest) three days and three nights after his death on the cross, 'he went and made proclamation to the imprisoned spirits – to those who were disobedient long ago when God waited patiently in the days of Noah while the ark was being built' 1Peter 3:19-20.

Another Greek word, translated as hell in most bibles is *Hades* from the Hebrew *Sheol*, which means a state of being dead. In Greek mythology hades is a place where the souls of dead people are alive and that belief spread among the Greek speaking world including the Jewish people. *Gehenna*, again, translated as hell, means the lake of fire that will destroy all the wicked on the Day of Judgment. Much confusion has been generated by translating these three very different words, *Tartarus, Gehenna, Hades* into the English word Hell. As well as completely ignoring the annual feast days of the Hebrews which enables us to see the chronology of Jesus' last week.

The writer of Hebrews says, 'If we deliberately keep on sinning after we have received the knowledge of the truth, no sacrifice for sins is left, but only a fearful expectation of judgment and of raging fire that will consume the enemies of God ... It is a dreadful thing to fall into the hands of the living God' Heb10: 26-27, 31. 'For our God is a consuming fire' 12:29. This restates what Moses wrote in Deuteronomy 4:24.

We need to move forward a thousand years after Jesus' return, and come to what is called, the second death. John, in his vision on the island of Patmos, records seeing 'the dead, great and small, standing before the throne, and books were opened. Another book was opened, which is the book of life. The dead were judged according to what they had done as recorded in the books. The sea gave up the dead that were in it, and death and Hades (state of being dead) gave up the dead that were in them, and everyone was judged according to what they had done. Then death and Hades were thrown into the lake of fire. The lake of fire is the second death. All whose names were not found written in the book of life were thrown into the lake of fire' Rev 20:12-15.

Not only has all that we have done been recorded but our motive and intent is also known. All have sinned, apart from Jesus – the only exception, Heb

4:15. 'Nothing in all creation is hidden from God's sight. Everything is uncovered and laid bare before the eyes of him to whom we must give account' Heb 4:13.

This is consistent with what Jeremiah wrote, 'I the Lord search the heart and examine the mind, to reward everyone according to their conduct, according to what their deeds deserve.' Jeremiah again, 'Am I only a God nearby, and not a God far away? Who can hide in secret places so that I cannot see them? Do I not fill heaven and earth?' Jer 17:10, 23:23-24.

David, in the psalms, said a similar thing, 'Where can I go from your spirit? Where can I flee from your presence? If I go up to the heavens, you are there; If I make my bed in the depths, you are there. If I rise on the wings of the dawn, if I settle on the far side of the sea, even there your hand will guide me, your right hand will hold me fast. If I say, surely the darkness will hide me and the light become night around me, even the darkness will not be dark to you; the night will shine like the day, for darkness is as light to you' Psa 139:7-12.

John wrote in his first letter, 'If we claim to be without sin, we deceive ourselves and the truth is not in us. If we confess our sins, he is faithful and just and will forgive us our sins and purify us from all unrighteousness. If we claim we have not sinned, we make him out to be a liar and his word is not in us' 1 John 1:8-10. Later in this letter he writes, 'Everyone who sins breaks the law; in fact, sin is lawlessness' 3:4. Paul wrote that 'the law is holy, and the commandment is holy, righteous and good ... we know that the law is spiritual; but I am unspiritual, sold as a slave to sin. I do not understand what I do. For what I want to do I do not do, but what I hate I do, and if I do what I do not want to do, I agree that the law is good. As it is, it is no longer I myself who do it, but it is sin living in me. I know that good itself does not dwell in me, that is, in my sinful nature. For I have the desire to do what is good, but I cannot carry it out' Rom 7:12-18.

This honest recognition of our sinful nature is something that we can all identify with, and our powerlessness to change it. Paul had written in an earlier section that 'just as sin entered the world through one man, and death through sin, and in this way death came to all people, because all sinned ...' Listen to how Paul explains the answer to sin and its deadly consequence. 'you see, at just the right time, when we were still powerless, Christ died for the ungodly. Very rarely will anyone die for a righteous person, though for a good person someone might possibly dare to die. But God demonstrates his own love for us in this: while we were still sinners, Christ died for us. Since we have now been justified by his blood, how much more shall we be saved from God's wrath through him. For if, while we were God's enemies, we were reconciled to him through the death of his Son, how much more, having been reconciled, shall we be saved through his life' Rom 5: 6-10.

Paul continues, 'Therefore, we have an obligation – but it is not to the sinful nature, to live according to it. For if you live according to the sinful nature, you will die; but if, by the spirit you put to death the misdeeds of the body, you will live. For those who are led by the spirit of God are the children of God' 8: 12-14.

'Therefore, (a favourite word of Paul's) there is no condemnation for those who are in Christ Jesus, because through Christ Jesus the law of the Spirit who gives life has set you free from the law of sin and death. For what the law was powerless to do because it was weakened by the sinful nature, God did by sending his own Son in the likeness of sinful humanity to be a sin offering, and so he condemned sin in human flesh, in order that the righteous requirement of the law might be fully met in us, who do not live according to the sinful nature but according to the Spirit. Those who live according to the sinful nature have their minds set on what that nature desires; but those who live in accordance with the Spirit have their minds set on what the Spirit desires. The mind controlled by the sinful nature is death, but the mind controlled by the Spirit is life and peace. The sinful mind is hostile to God; it does not submit to God's law, nor can it do so. Those controlled by the sinful nature cannot please God' Rom 8: 1-8.

Everyone has a conscience and knows what is good and what is evil. No one is condemned by what they did not know but what was in their heart – their motive and intent and how they lived in this dark and evil age.

Only God and Jesus can make such a judgment. For those who are sentenced to eternal death there will be the 'weeping and gnashing of teeth' that Jesus spoke about. They will respond in great distress and anger but then it will be too late.

'Then I saw a new heaven and a new earth, for the first heaven and the first earth had passed away, and there was no longer any sea. I saw the holy city, the new Jerusalem, coming down out of heaven from God, prepared as a bride beautifully dressed for her husband. And I heard a loud voice from the throne saying, 'Look! God's dwelling place is now among the people, and God himself will be with them and be their God. He will wipe every tear from their eyes. There will be no more death or mourning or crying or pain, for the old order of things has passed away.

'He who was seated on the throne said, 'I am making everything new!' then he said, 'Write this down, for the words are trustworthy and true.'

It would be close to impossible to get through April 2012 without the image of the Titanic grabbing our attention, one way or the other. Bookshops were displaying a wide choice of reading material on the disaster from personal recollections to all the technical aspects of the ship. James Cameron's highly successful film 'Titanic' was re-released with the addition of 3D, while ITV gave us a four-part drama of the sinking made during a hot summer where the actors couldn't wait to get into the water so that they could cool off. It was, for some, a relief when this strange obsession past. Yet the greatest maritime disaster in history with its 7,000 dead is hardly known.

For me, this came to light by reading Max Hasting's book 'Armageddon', covering the last six months of the Second World War. This specific event took place at the end of January 1945. The captain of the *Wilhelm Gustloff*, a 27,000-ton prewar Nazi cruise ship, was told to prepare to transport refugees westwards, away from the advancing Russian army. While money and influence gained many berths others like Stabsführein Wilhelmina Reitsch clamoured for space for some of the 8,000 naval auxiliaries in the port, whom she commanded. They were all girls between seventeen and twenty-five, acutely aware of their likely fate at the hands of the Russians. Only 373 were embarked. So were 918 naval personnel and 4,224 refugees.

For three days they waited in anguish in the crowded passenger decks for permission to sail. A special maternity unit was established on the sun deck, for some refugees who were heavily pregnant. One hundred and sixty-two military casualties, many of them amputees, were brought aboard on stretchers and placed in an emergency hospital. On the night of 27th January, the entire compliment was ordered ashore during an air raid. They spent hours of icy misery in the port's shelters, before they could board again at dawn.

On the 30th January, the morning of the ship's departure, military police boarded, to search for deserters. As the *Gustloff* finally cast off, a flotilla of small boats came alongside, filled with refugees begging to be taken aboard. Women holding high their babies. Compassionate crewmen let down scrambling nets. The manifest on 30th January showed more than 6,000 souls. Some 2,000 more are believed to have struggled aboard during the final rush. There was a further delay offshore, where the *Gustloff* anchored to await a second ship, the *Hansa.* Finally, the port authorities decided that it was too dangerous for the ship to wait. Escorted by a torpedo boat, the liner set course westwards. The *Hansa's* captain signalled: 'Bon voyage.'

A surge of relief swept through the decks of the *Gustloff.* At last, the passengers saw the prospect of safety after the terrors of the shore. A doctor persuaded a small orchestra to play for the military wounded. Unfortunately, the *Gustloff* began to wallow heavily in the Baltic chop. Ice formed on deck. Many, perhaps most, passengers were soon prostrate with sea-sickness. Some of those who had eaten dinner wished they had not.

Shortly before 7pm, between broken snow showers, thirty-three-year-old Captain Third Class Alexandr Marinesko of the soviet submarine *S-13* sighted a large ship, which to his amazement – as a result of German negligence – was not zigzagging and was showing lights. Now the *S-13* began to stalk the *Gustloff* on the surface, taking up a position down-moon, between ship and shore. It took him two hours to overhaul the liner and turn into a firing position. At 9.04, at point-blank range of less than a thousand yards, he fired a salvo of torpedoes, daubed with the usual slogans 'For the Motherland', 'Stalingrad', For the Soviet People'. There were three devastating explosions. The *Wilhelm Gustloff* listed heavily, and began to sink.

Most of the girl auxiliaries were killed instantly when a torpedo detonated below their living space. The old, the sick and wounded could not move, but perished more slowly. Most of the crew behaved contemptibly. A lifeboat with capacity for fifty pulled away carrying only the captain and twelve sailors. Another was lowered so recklessly that its load of passengers was upended into the sea. Several boats were never launched at all. The ship was soon lying broadside to the sea. It finally disappeared seventy minutes after the attack.

The *Gustloff*'s distress signal was heard by the heavy cruiser *Admiral Hipper*, which was also sailing that night with 1,377 refugees. As her course drove the cruiser past the grave of the liner, survivors struggling in the water waved frantically, clutching a moment of hope. The *Hipper*'s churning screws ended their suffering. The big warship could not risk heaving to, with a submarine close by. Alexandr Marinesko missed a far more useful target than the *Gustloff* that night. He never saw the *Hipper*.

The torpedo boat *T-36* was the only vessel to render immediate assistance. It was able to pick up 252 survivors. Many even among those who had found places in lifeboats froze to death before other rescuers arrived at daybreak. A naval petty officer who boarded one boat full of corpses next morning found an unidentified baby, blue with cold but still breathing. He adopted it. The child became one of just 949 known survivors of this maritime disaster.

There are many tragedies throughout history. Not all of them have been so well documented. Terrible events continue today and there is little evidence that anything will change.

Jesus was asked what was going to happen before his return and he told them that many would be deceived by a counterfeit religion that used his name but brought another message. He went on to say, 'You'll hear of wars and rumours of wars, but see to it that you're not alarmed. Such things must happen, but the end is still to come. Nation will rise against nation, and kingdom against kingdom. There will be famines and earthquakes in various places. All these are the beginning of birth-pains'.

Then he spoke of persecution and his people being put to death. People will turn away from the faith and betray and hate each other – false prophets will come and deceive many.

He later told them that they would be put out of the synagogue and that the time is coming when those who kill you will think they are offering a service to God. 'They will do such things because they have not known the Father or me'.

Part 7

Looking Back

W e need to go back to the beginning of church history if we are to make sense of the fractured and divided Christianity we see around us today.

The freedom to go to the church of our choosing, or not to go to church at all, is an experience unknown to earlier times when the state was involved with the church to a much greater level than it is today. Christendom did not allow diversity – unity was all. But behind the façade of unity there were divisions which had begun to rise even in the time of the apostles; the dragon did not lose any time.

Peter had warned, 'but there were also false prophets among the people (in the Old Testament period), just as there will be false teachers among you, 2 Peter 2:1. Paul, in speaking to the church leaders from Ephesus, told them, 'I know that after I leave, savage wolves will come in among you and will not spare the flock. Even from your own number men will arise and distort the truth in order to draw away disciples after them,' Acts 20:29-30.

Later, Paul writes to Timothy, saying, 'Preach the word; be prepared in season and out of season; correct, rebuke and encourage – with great patience and careful instruction. For the time will come when men will not put up with sound doctrine. Instead, to suit their own desires, they will gather around them a great number of teachers to say what their itching ears want to hear. They will turn their ears away from the truth and turn aside to myths' 2Tim 4:2-4.

Jesus said. '… and many false prophets will appear and deceive many people' Matt 24:11. In the same passage he said that 'false messiahs and false prophets will appear and preform great signs and miracles to deceive even the elect – if that were possible' verse 24.

The teachings established in the 4th and 5th centuries, as mandatory on all, were unnecessary and tragic in what they produced, although the creeds (summaries of belief) are considered by many as essential reminders of what is central to the church's teaching.

They were unnecessary because what they aggressively debated and stated as true was more philosophical than biblical. They were tragic because those who disagreed with the creeds were tagged as heretics and as such, enemies of the state.

We need to get an overview first. The Lion Handbook 'The History of Christianity' provides us with this. From the chapter, Councils and Creeds by David F. Wright, we read, 'The fourth, fifth and sixth centuries were marked by prolonged controversies, chiefly in the Eastern church. These were about how Christ, the Son of God, was himself God (the doctrine of the Trinity), and how he was both man and God.

Numerous councils of bishops were held. Four of them. Nicaea 325, Constantinople 381, Ephesus 431 and Chalcedon 451, came to be accepted as general or ecumenical (universal) councils, binding on the whole church. Some areas of Eastern Christianity rejected the decisions made at Ephesus and Chalcedon. Two later councils, at Constantinople in 553 and 680-81, dealt with similar questions. Many creeds and statements of doctrine were produced, including the famous Nicene Creed and the Chalcedonian Definition, which became touch-stones of orthodoxy throughout most of the Christian world.

At the same time it was an age of interference and even domination by the emperors, of colourful and abrasive personalities, and of bitter antagonism between leading bishoprics. Technical terms without biblical origins were made key-words in authoritative statements of belief. Their use contributed to the Latin-speaking West and the Greek-speaking East misunderstanding and misrepresenting one another. Even between different segments of the Greek church misunderstandings arose; these disputes contributed to major division in the Christian world.

In theory the first appeal was to Scripture, but the Bible was used in curious or questionable ways. People frequently appealed to Scripture to confirm their theology rather than to decide it. Above all, the disputes were shot through with the feeling that unless God and Christ were truly what Christian devotion and worship claimed, then salvation itself was endangered. Passions rang high because the fundamentals of the Christian religion were felt to be at stake.'

We are going to get into the details of church history, particularly with what happened in the 4th century, and some may feel that this has little or no connection with the challenge of being a Christian in today's world yet that would be to ignore that we owe our foundational teachings to what was decided at that time, and if what was decreed as definitive is then found to be faulty, a radical rethinking of our core beliefs needs to be addressed.

The emperor Constantine is considered as the

protector and promoter of Christianity throughout the empire. His firm aim was to achieve unity and conformity, and so bring about a settled and peaceful empire.

Ivor J. Davidson, in his book, 'A Public Faith' volume two of the Monarch History of the Church, writes, 'the story that Constantine experienced a vision of the cross in the sky prior to the battle at the Milvian Bridge is in other versions presented as a vision of the pagan Sun-god. He retained the pagan title of *Pontifex Maximus* and did little if anything to curtail the imperial cult. The coins Constantine issued in his early years as emperor included images of *Sol Invictus*, 'the Unconquered Sun' (as well as symbols of other various other pagan gods), and the still extant triumphal arch later erected in Rome to celebrate his victory over Maxentius also depicts *Sol Invictus* as Constantine's protector, referring simply to 'the divinity' unspecified. When in 321 he declared the first day of the week (Sunday) a public holiday, his stated reason was to respect 'the venerable day of the Sun.'

It was the emperor Aurelian, who reigned from 270-275, that decreed 25th December as the birthday of *Sol Invictus* which was a welcome addition to the seven-day period of *Saturnalia* which was celebrated with parties, banquets and exchanges of gifts.

Ever since the great persecution, which begun under Diocletian in 303 and lasted until 312, the churches in the north of Africa had been faced with dissension. This had happened before. On January 3rd 250 the emperor Decius performed the annual sacrifice to Jupiter and the Roman gods in the Capitoline temple in Rome and he delivered an edict that similar sacrifices be offered throughout the empire. If Christians did not obey the command to sacrifice, they would be regarded as political subversives, guilty not only of disobedience to the law but of offending the gods and jeopardizing the unity of the empire. The penalty for such behaviour was death.

Decius had launched the first systematic and empire-wide attack on the Christians since the beginnings of the church. It did not last long because Decius was killed fighting the Goths, and in June 251 his religious policy was ended, but the effect on the church was considerable and lasting. While the edict stood the Christians had to obtain a special certificate, or *libellous*, proving that the statutory sacrifice had been performed in the presence of designated officials. A commission was established in each city, and every individual had to obtain its signature, certifying that the sacrifice had duly taken place, accompanied by a cultic libation and eating of the sacrificial meat.

All over the empire there was a rush to comply. In Carthage, the crowds queued up in such numbers at the temples to collect their piece of paper that the system could hardly cope. In Smyrna, the bishop. Euctemon, led his congregation in person to the temple, and it was much the same in many other places. There was widespread acquiescence, especially from those who risked the confiscation of their property. Some believers were able to get away and go into hiding, such as the bishops Cyprian of Carthage and Dionysius of Alexandria, who ministered to their congregations from exile by secret correspondence.

Others managed to bribe less hostile commissioners to give them certificates stating that they had sacrificed when they had not. This practice was frowned on by Christian leaders, but in the aftermath of the troubles those who had resorted to this expedient were considered to be somewhat better than those who had given in and obeyed the law. A few bravely held out and paid the ultimate price, such as an elder in Smyrna named Pionius and a small group of his followers, who all refused to copy their bishop and yield to the authorities despite appeals not to throw their lives away. Overall, however, the number of deaths was low – confronted with the choice of obeying Christ or the emperor, a large majority of believers, including a great many of their leaders, took the easy way out.

The issue then dividing Christians was the status of those who had weakened during the persecution. There was a good deal of disorganization. Some bishops treated the lapsed more leniently than others. Those who had suffered imprisonment, torture, and privation for resisting the authorities were to be considered to be 'confessors' – people who had held tenaciously to their beliefs under severe pressure. In Carthage, the fugitive bishop Cyprian found on his return in 251 that his church was dominated by confessors. He had suffered a serious loss of public esteem in his absence, and Christians who had formerly been incarcerated had usurped his authority. The confessors, held by many to be specially anointed by the Holy Spirit, were taking it upon themselves to sign certificates authorizing the clergy to restore transgressors to communion. Cyprian was simply expected to endorse their decisions. Leniency was to be the order of the day.

Things finally came to a head in 311 with the election of the moderate clergyman Caecilian as bishop of Carthage.

Opponents of Caecilian, known as Donatists, claimed that his election was invalid, since he had been consecrated by a person who had handed over his copy of the scriptures to be burned during the persecutions. The Donatists, mostly from the rural areas of modern-day Eastern Algeria, called a synod of 70 bishops and announced that Caecilian had been deposed. In his place they ordained Majorinus, who died shortly after and was replaced by Donatus, after whom the movement is named. He insisted that the true church was to be found among those who had maintained a steadfast testimony in the face of oppression. Caecilian and his supporters did not recognise the authority of the synod. So Carthage had two bishops, and the church was threatened with a full-blown schism.

The Donatists took their case to Constantine and an imperial commission decided against Donatus – Caecilian was backed and Donatus ruled against.

In 316 Constantine heard a further appeal by the Donatists and once more he backed Caecilian. Constantine saw himself as more than a secular emperor – he was God's emissary, empowered to unify his church. Between 317 and 321 many

Donatists were killed. The Roman state found itself once again the persecutor, but this time it was in the name of Christianity.

The difficulties suffered by the Donatists only intensified their resolve and they considered that they were the real people of God, prepared to pay the price for their faith. The Donatists schism would completely dominate North African church life for well over a century. The Donatists survived for three centuries, despite intermittent attempts to root them out – they only disappeared with the obliteration of Christianity in North Africa after the Muslim conquest.

Augustine of Hippo, 354-430, became ever more prepared to ask for and justify the use of force to deal with the Donatists. Hippo was a seaport in Algeria. 'Coercion,' Augustine said, 'could even be presented as obedience to the Lord's command to 'compel them to come in'' Luke 14:23. He depicted the fate inflicted upon the Donatists as a matter of spiritual discipline, a harsh but necessary infliction laid upon them with a positive end in mind.

Augustine's attempts to defend his conduct may reflect his efforts to rationalize it to himself. Sometimes, he argued, punishment and fear might move people to repentance in ways love and patience do not. In later years it was clearly all too easy for an influential churchman to mobilize the forces of law and order to enforce a particular ecclesiastic position. Whatever the complexities of Augustine's own case against the Donatists, his stance served ever after as an example to which some of the European churches' darker tacticians might appeal, and in the medieval, Reformation, and Counter-Reformation periods legitimacy would be sought for more than a few programs of brutal repression by citing Augustine's moves against the Donatists.

Meanwhile, in the East an even greater dispute was threatening to divide the church.

Part 8

Church & State

T his time the dispute was not about ecclesiastical discipline but about the person of Christ himself. Once again, Constantine found himself embroiled in a heated debate within the church. At the centre of this argument was Arius, an intelligent, independent and popular elder in Alexandria. Like his predecessor Origen and other Christian theologians, Arius differed with numerous believers over the nature of the Son of God and his exact relationship to God his Father.

The details of Arius's own position, both at this stage and later on, are difficult to uncover, as much of the documentation comes from those who were his opponents, then or later. They naturally had their own reasons for presenting his ideas in a negative way. Even the writings that did survive by Arius himself – a couple of letters and some fragments of a poem – survive because they were deliberately selected by his critics to show up his views in the worst possible light. Often Arius is alleged to have held opinions and said things that he probably did not. Some of the diverse forms of what came to be known as Arianism that developed during the 4th century were far removed from the teachings of Arius himself.

Arius's enemies depicted him as a devious philosopher, led astray by his fondness for subtle, logical analysis. Yet Arius saw himself as a conservative, holding to the doctrinal traditions he had inherited, and seeking to anchor them in biblical texts rather than, as was popular then, speculative metaphysics.

Many of the leaders of that time went beyond what they read in the scriptures and looked to philosophy to fill in any gaps they felt that scripture did not adequately explain.

Arius wrote to Alexander, bishop of Alexandria, setting out his views on God. He presented himself as following the traditions in which he had been taught and seeking to be obedient to his bishop. He claimed to believe in God, the Father, who alone is unbegotten, alone everlasting … The Son is God's offspring, begotten of the unbegotten, and thus a creature; he is not *homoousios*, 'of one substance,' with the Father. On the basis of this teaching, Alexander initiated action against Arius, and he and his supporters were under the serious disapproval of their bishop.

Arius contacted Eusebius, bishop of Nicomedia (there were three other bishops named Eusebius in that period!) complaining that he had not been treated fairly by Alexander. Eusebius was close to the imperial court and was in an important position to support Arius's cause, and he was successful in leading others to be sympathetic to his ideas. Arius also appealed to other clergy, protesting his orthodoxy.

Alexander, for his part, issued an encyclical letter, informing the churches that Arius had been condemned by the bishops of Egypt and Libya. Alexander insisted that Arius's teaching was seriously in error. Formally excommunicated, Arius and a group of his supporters were obliged to leave their churches. However, Arius continued to write to other churchmen, and his support grew. His most powerful church advocate was the bishop of Caesarea, Eusebius, who put himself into serious trouble by speaking on behalf of Arius.

By late 324 the churches of the East were sharply divided between those who sided with Arius and those who supported Alexander. Constantine attempted to settle the matter by writing to both Alexander and Arius, urging them to put behind them the apparently trivial issues that had led to their dispute, 'Give me back peaceful nights and days without care,' he wrote, 'that I to may keep some pleasure in the pure light and the joy of a tranquil life henceforth.' He also wrote that the excommunication of Arius and his fellow clergy remained valid and could only be revoked by the emperor's permission.

Constantine's response to this dispute was, as Edward Gibbon writes in his 'The Decline and Fall of the Roman Empire', 'to a trifling and subtle question concerning an incomprehensible point of the law, which was foolishly asked by the bishop and imprudently resolved by the presbyter.' Gibbon goes on, 'Constantine laments that the Christian people, who had the same God, the same religion, and the same worship, should be divided by such inconsiderable distinctions; and he seriously recommends to the clergy of Alexandria the example of the Greek philosophers, who could maintain their arguments without losing their temper, and assert their freedom without violating their friendship.'

The letter was dispatched to Alexander and Arius by Ossius, the bishop of Cordoba, who pressed the view that while tolerance and forgiveness were necessary, Arius was in the end obliged to respect the authority of the bishop and submit to his discipline.

Early in 325 a synod at Antioch elected a staunch opponent of Arius, Eustarthius, as the new bishop of Antioch and he declared the belief that the distinction of being the Son of God did not mean that the Son was a created being. The Son must not be thought of as having a beginning. Three bishops dissented from this position, one of whom was Eusebius of Caesarea. They were provisionally excommunicated, pending ratification of the judgment at the council to be held at Ancyra in Galatia – modern Ankara in Turkey – a few weeks later.

Constantine was eager to see a settlement to the doctrinal wrangling. The dispute that had started in Alexandria was not only undermining ecclesiastical relations throughout the East but was quite capable of spreading towards the West and making mockery of his dream of an empire unified theologically as well as politically.

The venue for the council was changed to Nicaea. It was just across the Bosphorus and would be more accessible for Western churchmen.

The Council of Nicaea convened on May 20, 325. It assembled not on church property but in an imperial building, and Constantine himself chaired the opening session. Eusebius recalled in his biography of Constantine, like 'some heavenly messenger of God, clothed in a shining raiment, which flashed with glittering rays of light.'

It was the largest gathering of churchmen called up to that time. The total number of bishops present was probably around 220, all of them transported, housed and fed at public expense in accordance with Constantine's policy of granting benefits to the clergy. The great majority of them were from the East. The handful of Westerners included Ossius of Cordoba and two presbyters sent by bishop Sylvester of Rome. The open supporters of Arius perhaps numbered about 20 in all. After Constantine had solemnly exhorted the delegates to reach an agreement, he handed over the formal presidency of the council to Ossius. The emperor had stamped his authority upon the occasion from the start, and none of the participants was unaware of his determination that a solution be found to the crisis that Arius had started.

The deliberations at Nicaea went on for two months. No precise record of the details, official or private, have come down to us, and our knowledge of what happened must be pieced together from various kinds of later evidence. It appears to have been decided quite early on that the theology of Arius and his followers was unacceptable. But they did need to find a clear statement of faith. The fundamental feature of God, they held, is his unity, and the distinction between the Father and the Son is essentially a temporal one relative to creation.

The challenge lay in trying to come up with a statement that would express the relationship of the Father and the Son in a way that neither reduced the divinity of the Son nor rendered the distinction between the Father and the Son merely a matter of temporal manifestations.

It is worth noting that what they were attempting went beyond and outside of what the Bible does reveal of the reality of God. The Bible uses both analogy and metaphor in describing things of the Spirit because we have serious limits to what we can comprehend. God's concern for human kind is revealed in his words and actions, yet, when Jesus said, to the woman at the well, 'God is spirit, and his worshippers must worship in spirit and in truth'. God is invisible to us and his reality is beyond our human capabilities to fully understand, but his nature and heart is made clear in the scriptures, and supremely. in the life and teaching of Jesus. 'God is love' John wrote, 'Whoever lives in love lives in God, and God in them' 1John 4:16. 'For now we see only a reflection as in a mirror; then we shall see face to face. Now I know in part; then I shall know fully, even as I am fully known' 1Cor 13;12. 'The throne of God and of the Lamb will be in the city, and his servants will serve him. They will see his face …' Rev 22:3-4.

To attempt to formalise a statement outside of Scripture and based on speculation, which would be made mandatory on all Christians, would compound an error into a state crime against all who disagreed.

Eusebius of Caesarea presented a creed of his own to the council for approval, claiming that it represented his traditional position – it was, he said, the creed he had professed at baptism and had always taught as a churchman. Part of Eusebius's creed affirmed belief in the Son as the Only-begotten of the Father, to be spoken of as 'God from God, light from light, life from life, Only-begotten Son, firstborn of all creation, before all ages begotten from the Father …' Eusebius himself, in his book *Ecclesiastical History*, tells us that Constantine expressed his approval of this language and proposed that it would be adopted, with the addition of the word *homoousios* (of one substance) to describe the relationship of the Son to the Father's divinity.

Eusebius's evidence is naturally concerned to justify its author's stance and to magnify the part played by Constantine, who wisely recognised truth when he heard it. The creed Eusebius proposed in defence of his orthodoxy was not his creation but was rooted in an existing Palestinian or Syrian tradition. There were subtle but important differences between the wording of Eusebius's creed and the statement that was finally adopted at Nicaea, and Eusebius was only able to agree to the final Nicene formula after considerable evasion.

In the end, the following definition was proposed:

We believe in one God, the Father Almighty, Maker of all things visible and invisible

And in one Lord Jesus Christ, the Son of God, begotten of the Father, Only-begotten, that is, from the substance [ousia] of the Father; God from God, Light from Light, true God from true God, begotten not made, of one substance [*homoousios*] with the Father, by whom all things were made; who for us human beings and for our salvation came down and was incarnate, was made human, suffered, and rose again the third day, ascended into heaven, and is coming to judge the living and the dead.

And in the Holy Spirit.

After these clauses, the following statements were added:

And those who say, 'There was when he was not,' and 'Before his generation he was not,' and 'He came to be from nothing,' or those who pretend that the Son of God is of other reality [hypostasis] or substance [*ousia*] the catholic and apostolic church anathematizes.

What is read and spoken today as the Nicene Creed comes from the Council of Constantinople in 381. In January 438 an edict was issued from Thessalonica by the emperor Theodosius to the people of Constantinople:

'It is Our will that all peoples ruled by the administration of Our Clemency shall practice that religion which the divine Peter the Apostle transmitted to the Romans ... this is the religion followed by bishop Damasus of Rome and by Peter, bishop of Alexandria, a man of apostolic sanctity: that is, according to the apostolic discipline of the evangelical doctrine, we shall believe in the single deity of the Father, the Son and the Holy Ghost under the concept of equal majesty and of the Holy Trinity.

We command that persons who follow this rule shall embrace the name of catholic Christians. The rest, however, whom We judge demented and insane, shall carry the infamy of heretical dogmas. Their meeting places shall not receive the name of churches, and they shall be smitten first by Divine Vengeance, and secondly by the retribution of hostility which We shall assume in accordance with the Divine Judgement.'

The word *homoousios*, that Eusebius claimed Constantine had suggested, is a word with a difficult history. For a start, it was not biblical, which meant that the council was talking about the nature of God in terms that were philosophical rather than in language drawn directly from the scriptures.

For Arius and those sympathetic to him, this was a serious problem, for they believed sound theology ought to use the language of the Bible. First introduced into theological discussion by Gnostic teachers to describe the way in which heavenly powers participated in the fullness of God, *homoousios* had been employed in the 260s by Libyan bishops whom Dionysius of Alexandria had condemned and by Paul of Samosata, who was condemned by the Council of Antioch in 268 for so stressing the oneness of God that he denied the pre-existence of the Son.

The outcome of the council was close to being unanimous. All but two of the bishops agreed to sign the creed. Those two, as well as Arius, were exiled and the rest appeared to be at one, and Constantine had got his way.

The reality was far more complex. This important word *homoousios* could in fact be understood in a variety of ways. For the enemies of Arius, *homoousios* meant 'one and the same being' but for Eusebius of Caesarea it meant 'exactly like in being' – potentially a very significant difference. Is the Son *the same as* God in his being, or is he *exactly like* God in his being?

To modern readers, the complex and strange-sounding slogans bandied about in the fourth century can seem like an absurd game of words, in which theologians split hairs about the inscrutable mysteries of God's inner being. The great eighteenth-century historian of the later Roman Empire, Edward Gibbon, famously characterized the differences between the *homoosians* and the *homoiousians* as the division of Christendom over an iota. How could it possible matter that much whether the Son of God was confessed to be 'identical' to God the Father or simply 'like' God in his essence?

Gibbon thought debates of this kind merely illustrated the absurdities and intolerance of early Christian reasoning. But even those who had no wish to dismiss the importance of orthodox tradition may find the technicalities over which the bishops argued to be bizarre. It suggests that the real Jesus they all claimed to have experienced had been forgotten.

Other issues dealt with at Nicaea included the question of the date of Easter, which had been a matter of significant controversy since the second century. This issue was called the '*Quartodeciman*' question. The word Easter goes back to the Saxon for the spring festival in honour of the goddess of the dawn, Eostre or Ostara and would have had traditional symbols for that period, such as eggs, baby animals and new flowers.

Part 9

Passover & Easter

L iberation came to the enslaved people of Israel on the 15th Nisan, the first month in their calendar. The evening before, each family, in their own homes, had killed a lamb that they had with them since the 10th of that month. The animal was a year-old male without any defect. It was to be slaughtered at twilight. Before it was cooked and eaten some of its blood was smeared over the tops and sides of their door-frames. As they ate the meal they were fully dressed and ready to leave their homes at dawn.

This was the 13th century B.C. The twelve tribes of Israel, all descended from Jacob, were about to leave Egypt. Moses, who was a Levite, had told the leaders of Israel that none of them must leave their homes until morning. When the death angel goes through the land to kill the Egyptians he will see the blood on the top and sides of the door-frames and will pass over that entrance and God will not allow the destroyer to enter and kill anyone inside.

'Obey these instructions', Moses told them, as a lasting ordinance for them and their descendants.

At midnight all the firstborn in Egypt, from the firstborn of Pharaoh, who sat on the throne, to the firstborn of the prisoner, who was in the dungeon, and the firstborn of all the livestock as well. Pharaoh and all his officials and all Egyptians got up during the night, and there was a loud crying in Egypt, because there was not a house that did not have someone dead.

During that night Pharaoh summoned Moses and Aaron and ordered them to leave and go and worship your God as they had requested. 'Take your flocks and herds, as you have said, and go. And also bless me.'

The Egyptians urged the people to leave as quickly as possible as they thought that they were all going to die. The Israelites took their dough before the yeast was added and carried it on their shoulders in kneading troughs wrapped in clothing. They did as Moses instructed and asked the Egyptians for silver and gold and for clothing. The Egyptians were eager to give the Israelites all they asked for and they took as much as they wanted.

Counting the number of men aged twenty and over, Judah had the largest number: 74,000. The total number of Israelite men who left Egypt was 603,550, not counting the women and children. Moses records that many other people went with them as well.

It is a common assumption that the Israelites were all Jews. Even Charlton Heston, who played Moses, said somewhere about saving the Jews in the film 'The Ten Commandments'. The nation of Israel, at that time, were the descendants of the twelve sons of Jacob: Reuben, Simeon, Levi, Judah, Dan, Naphtali, Gad, Asher, Issachar, Zebulun and Joseph and Benjamin. Joseph's two sons, Ephraim and Manasseh became two tribes. When they entered Canaan they were each allotted an area to settle on except Levi who were not given any land as they were to be priests who lived throughout the land. The Jews were the descendants of Judah. From being one nation they became divided – Judah against Israel, often at war with each other. The first mention of Jews in the AV is found in 2 Kings 16:6 where we read that Israel was allied with Syria in fighting against the Jews.

That unique night of deliverance from slavery was of great significance, not only in the history of Israel but also to Christians, who saw in the sheading of the lamb's blood, the shed blood of the

Messiah Jesus, as John the Baptist said, 'Look, the Lamb of God, who takes away the sin of the world.' And Paul, who wrote, 'For Christ, our Passover lamb, has been sacrificed. Therefore let us keep the festival, not with the old bread leavened with malice and wickedness, but with the unleavened bread of sincerity and truth, John 1:29, 1Cor 5:7-8.

For seven days following the Passover the Israelites were to eat unleavened bread, Lev 23:6-8. The first and last day of that seven-day period where to be holy days: annual sabbaths.

Acts 20:6 tells us of Paul sailing from Phillippi after the Feast of Unleavened Bread. Those special days had not been forgotten.

The prophet Isaiah had written, 'He was oppressed and afflicted, yet he did not open his mouth; he was led like a lamb to the slaughter ...' Isa 53:7.

Peter wrote, '... with the precious blood of Christ, a lamb without blemish or defect', 1Peter 1:19.

The Passover and the other festivals continued to be kept in Judea until the war with Rome and the destruction of Jerusalem in A.D.70.

The controversy over when, or if, to keep

the Passover was called the 'Quartodeciman' (fourteenth) dispute. Churches in the eastern part of the Roman empire traditionally continued to observe the Passover on the fourteenth of Nisan, regardless of which day that date fell on. In Rome, the *Pascha* was not held annually until perhaps 160, but when it was kept, it was celebrated on the Sunday following the Jewish Passover.

Eusebius tells us that Polycarp travelled to Rome in his old age (in 154 or 155) to discuss with the Roman bishop, Anicetus, a number of matters concerning the observance of Easter, including the question of its date. At this stage, annual observance in Rome was still not the norm, and Anicetus followed the principle that the Lord's resurrection was celebrated every Sunday rather than once a year. The meeting produced no agreement, but they parted on good terms and pledged to respect each other's positions.

In the eastern areas of the church they retained the tradition of the fourteenth-day practice. Around 170 bishop Melito of Sardis gave a sermon about how the sacrifice of Jesus was a fulfilment of deliverance typified by the Hebrew Passover. His appeal was not to the continuity between Christianity and Judaism but to the absolute superiority of Christ over the sacrifices of Jewish religious practice, which the letter to the Hebrews, chapters 8-10 would agree with, but Melito issued a bitter attack on Judaism, blaming 'ungrateful Israel' for its crime in failing to recognise the Messiah and in orchestrating his crucifixion. The tone of his rhetoric marked a low point in early Christian antisemitism.

A generation after Anicetus had agreed to disagree with Polycarp, Victor, bishop of Rome aroused considerable opposition by attempting to impose uniformity of practice for all the churches. Victor, the first Latin-speaking bishop of Rome, called on all churches to follow Romes lead by observing Easter on the Sunday after Passover. He called synods, regional councils of bishops in Rome, Palestine and elsewhere and threatened to excommunicate all communities that refused to comply. When congregations in Asia Minor refused to follow his edict, he excommunicated them. Polycrates, the bishop of Ephesus, wrote to Victor, saying, 'I am not scared of threats.'

Irenaeus who, while keeping to the Roman practice himself, argued that Victor's injunction was an abuse of authority that would needlessly divide the churches. Irenaeus's counsel prevailed, and Victor countermanded his excommunication order. In the long term, the position sponsored by Victor would win out, and the Council of Nicaea in

325 would stipulate that Easter should be celebrated everywhere as a Sunday festival.

In his book, 'Constantine's Sword' James Carroll writes, 'The triumphalism of an empowered Christianity led to a betrayal of faith that all of pagan Rome's legions had failed to bring about. And what reveals that betrayal so clearly, of course, is the church's relations with the Jews. It was at Nicaea – the city named for Nike, the goddess of victory – at the council enshrining the Christian victory, that Constantine, forbidding the observance of Easter at Passover time, declared, 'It is unbecoming that on the holiest of festivals we should follow the customs of the Jews; henceforth let us have nothing in common with this odious people.'

Later, Carroll writes, 'The fluidity of interaction between these groups (Jews and Christians) is reflected in the ways that church fathers, well into the fourth century, warn against Christian participation in Jewish observances. For centuries, Christians' celebration of Easter coincided exactly with Passover, and their observance with the Sabbath continued to take place on Saturday. It took an order of Constantine, referred to earlier, and decrees of the fourth-century Church councils to draw fast distinctions between Jewish and Christian observances, but the purpose of such decrees was to clarify the minds of Christians, who continued to think of themselves as Jewish.'

In Catherine Nixey's book 'The Darkening Age' she makes the same point: 'There was little interest in Hebrew writings by now. According to the hectoring sermons being preached by a new generation of intolerant Christian clerics, the Jews were not a people with an ancient wisdom to be learnt from: they were instead, like the pagans, the hated enemies of the church. A few years earlier, the preacher John Chrysostom had said that: the synagogue is not only a brothel … it is also a den of robbers and a lodging of wild beasts … a dwelling of demons … a place of idolatry'. Chrysostom's writings would later be reprinted with enthusiasm in Nazi Germany.'

Through condemned by various church councils, Those still observing the 14th Nisan for Passover services were to be found in many places in the East for several centuries.

The Quartodeciman position was almost certainly the more ancient practice, but it lost out to sheer force of custom, reinforced by the weight of Rome's authority. It showed how seriously Rome regarded its right to impress its views on believers elsewhere and how determined a forceful bishop could be in asserting such a position.

Ivor J. Davidson, in his first of his two volumes of church history, has provided me with much of the material I have used here, as well as other historians. Davidson had made an important point that has been with us throughout the history of the church, 'The early second century self-defining of Christianity took place in part amid a strengthening vilification of Judaism that would have appalled earlier leaders of the Jesus movement. Within a short period of time, the seeds would be sown that would be developed into the shocking traditions of Christian antisemitism, in which the Jews would be blamed directly for the crucifixion of the Messiah and regarded as apostates upon whom God's judgment had justly fallen.'

Charles Freeman writes in his book 'The Closing of the Western Mind' 'The resurrection was believed to have taken place on the day of the sun, the most important day of the week for Christian worship (as the English word Sunday still suggests). A third-century fresco from the Vatican Hill in Rome even shows Christ dressed as the sun-god in a chariot on the way to heaven. The Christian writer Lactantius, who was writing at this time, urged Christians to observe the sun as if it were heaven and a symbol of 'the perfect majesty and might and splendour' of God. 'It is likely', concludes J.W. Liebeschuetz in his perceptive study of Constantine's proclamations, *Change and Continuity in Roman Religion*, 'that in the minds of many fringe Christians, Jesus and the sun were closely associated.' In the fifth century Pope Leo was to rebuke Christians at St Peter's for turning their backs on St Peter's tomb and standing on the front steps of the basilica to worship the rising sun. Remarkably, the main festival of *Sol Invictus* was on the day of the winter solstice, 25 December, adopted by Christians in the fourth century as the birthday of Christ.'

Gore Vidal in his book 'Julian' has the young Julian (who became emperor in 361) listening to his Bishop, Eusebius, tell him, 'All you need to know is that your cousin, the emperor, is a devout and good man, and never forget that you are at his mercy.' The Bishop then made me recite for four hours, as punishment for imprudence. But the lesson I learned was not the one intended. All that I understood was that Constantius was a devout Christian. Yet he had killed his own flesh and blood, Therefore, if he could be both a good

Christian and a murderer, then there was something wrong with his religion.'

When we reject Passover on the grounds that it is Jewish and accept Easter as Christian then perhaps there is something wrong with our religion. Vidal, through Julian, says, 'The Christians do not offer enough, though I must say they are outrageously bold in the way they adapt our most sacred rituals and festivals to their own ends.'

Part 10

Arius & Athanasius

The Council of Nicaea ended in late July 325 with a banquet to celebrate the twentieth year of Constantine's reign. The dispute between Alexander and Arius was settled, but it did not take long before the cracks to appear in the unity that Constantine prided himself on having secured. A matter of weeks later, Eusebius of Nicomedia, having signed the creed (he had campaigned aggressively on behalf of Arius and signed the creedal statement only under coercion from Constantine himself) he extended communion to Arius who had been condemned by the council. There was similar behaviour from Theognis, another signatory and the bishop of Nicaea!

Constantine was outraged: their actions were, in his mind, political treason as well as doctrinally deceitful. The two senior bishops were removed from their posts by imperial command and sent into exile. They appealed, protesting that they had, after all, agreed to the Creed of Nicaea, and at a meeting of a church court around 328 the decision was reversed, with the emperor's approval.

Meanwhile, Arius had sent a statement of his faith to Constantine in which he said his beliefs were scriptural and traditional. At the same meeting that reinstated Eusebius and Theognis, Arius's plea was accepted, and he was recalled from exile.

Constantine wrote to the bishop of Alexandria and explained how Arius had repented; 'I tell you that Arius, *the* Arius, came to me, the Augustus, on the recommendations of many persons, promising that he believed our Catholic faith which was decided and confirmed at the Council of Nicaea.' Satisfied that Arius was truly sincere he was readmitted. Perhaps Constantine was influenced by his mother, half-sister, and sister-in-law, who were all pro-Arian.

In Egypt, Alexander ignored the order to readmit Arius to communion, and when Alexander died in April 328 the request went unanswered. His successor, a young man by the name of Athanasius, did not want Arius readmitted as he had been condemned for heresy, and as far as Athanasius was concerned the charge was just and would remain.

Athanasius is considered by many as a spiritual giant and a champion of orthodoxy. Others believe he was a cunning political strategist who was not adverse to using extreme measures, including violence to achieve his goals. He was incapable of compromise and believed that anyone who disagreed with him was not only wrong but also evil. In his lifelong battle against Arianism, he never shied away from conflict with anyone who sided with Arius, even the emperor himself. Constantine wrote threatening to depose and exile him if he did not agree to readmit Arius to the church, but Athanasius never wavered in his defence of the full divinity of Christ. The charges against him of coercion and intimidation did have some substance, and the combined influence of Eusebius of Nicomedia and others meant that he was subject to investigation.

By 335 Constantine was in a mood to reconcile Arian sympathizers. Encouraged by the Eusebians, he worked for the restoration of all the supporters of Arius as the way to bring peace to his empire. The opportunity to do this would be the dedication of the great new Church of the Resurrection in Jerusalem. He invited churchmen from all over the empire, and those who would oppose reconciliation needed to be dealt with first.

At a meeting of bishops in Tyre in 335, presided over by an imperial official, the Eusebian party secured condemnation of Athanasius for conduct unbecoming a bishop; he was disposed from his see and excommunicated. His crimes had nothing to do formally with his doctrinal position; they lay squarely in his moral behaviour.

Athanasius, knowing he was heavily outnumbered by his adversaries, had expected to be condemned, and he appealed in person to Constantine, who had meanwhile gone ahead with his dedication ceremony in Jerusalem. At first the emperor was inclined to take his side, but he was induced to believe that the Alexandrian church would be better off without him, so he decided to banish the troublesome bishop to Trier in Gaul; Athanasius had threatened to call a dock strike in Alexandria to disrupt the vital grain supply from Egypt to Constantinople if he did not get his way.

It has been written that Athanasius industriously removed from Christology every trace of Judaism, and applied 'Jewishness' to his opponents as a sort of villainous moniker to discredit their positions. There was an active push to separate Christians from the unique God of the Jews.

Richard E. Rubenstein says, in his book 'When Jesus became God', 'the real thrust of the Cappadocian doctrine was to differentiate the Christian 'Godhead,' which now incorporated

Jesus and the Holy Spirit, from the monolithic God worshipped by Jews, radical Arians, and, later on, by Muslims, Unitarians, Bahais, and others ... Christians who accepted this triune God, distributed over three Persons, no longer shared Jehovah with their Jewish forebears or the Supreme Being with their pagan neighbours, nor could Jews or pagans claim to believe in the same God as that worshipped by the Christians. Doctrinally, this is the point at which Christianity breaks decisively with its parent faith and with other forms of monotheism.'

When in 337 Constantine realised he was dying, it was Eusebius of Nicomedia who baptised him. He survived his emperor by only four years. In 341, the year of his death, Eusebius consecrated the 30-year-old Wulfila, a missionary to the Goths of Dacia, north of the Danube, as the first bishop of the Goths. This act had far-reaching consequences, for when the descendants of Wulfila's followers invaded the West three generations later, they took Wulfila's Arianism with them, and it constituted a major stumbling block to Christian unity until the time of Charlemagne.

As the early history of both Donatism and Arianism showed, the decisions of church leaders on matters of the faith were now bound up as never before with the whims and stratagems of secular authority, and the process of framing statements of Christian beliefs was capable of being powerfully influenced by political interests, often regardless of biblical or spiritual considerations.

When Christians disagreed about issues of belief and practice, their appeals to the state could mean serious trouble for those who lost out in the competition for the emperor's favour. The dangers of intolerance and the incentive to impose uniformity rather than negotiate differences were given impetus such as had not existed in earlier ages.

In 341 a group of Eastern bishops assembled at Antioch to celebrate the completion of a great new church, the 'golden' basilica, which had been begun by Constantine and was now, at last, ready to be dedicated under Constantius. At that time they declared their fidelity to the theology of 'one only-begotten Son of God' who 'before all ages subsisted and coexisted with the Father who begot him.' The Holy Spirit was declared to be a third *hypostasis*, genuinely distinct from the Father and the Son.

To many Christian leaders in the West, this stance adopted at Antioch was highly suspicious. The Eastern bishops may have claimed to be anti-Arian, but they made no mention of Nicaea's most difficult word, *homoousios*, 'of identical substance.' This can easily be confused with *homoiousios*, 'of like substance.' And that infamous 'i' was a serious point of difference between the bishops.

Another contentious issue coming out of Antioch was the talk of 'three *hypostaseis*,' translated into Latin, it sounded like a belief in three gods, for it came out literally, as 'three *substantiae*.' Were the Eastern leaders not close to a belief in three gods rather than one?

Hilary, who became bishop of Poitiers around 350, had spent four years in exile in Phrygia and while there he came into contact with the debates over Arian theology. When he returned to the West in 360, Hilary spoke out against the teachings of Arius, so much so, that he was given the title of 'the Athanasius of the West'. Hilary's comment on the various debates and creeds is interesting: 'It is a thing equally deplorable and dangerous, that there are as many creeds as opinions among men, as many doctrines as inclinations, and as many sources of blasphemy as there are faults among us; because we make creeds arbitrarily, and explain them arbitrarily. The homoousion is rejected, and received, and explained away by successive synods. The partial or total resemblance of the Father and of the Son is a subject of dispute for these unhappy times. Every year, nay, every moon, we make new creeds to describe invisible mysteries. We repent of what we have done, we defend those who repent, we anathematise those whom we have defended. We condemn either the doctrine of others in ourselves, or our own in that of others, and, reciprocally tearing one another to pieces, we have been the cause of each other's ruin.'

At this distance in time, the theological issue in the Arian controversy may seem to have been merely a matter of semantics. But in fact it touched the very heart of Christianity at a moment when the church was struggling to satisfy two distinct needs. On the one hand, the church had given the world a monotheistic religion available to everybody; on the other hand, it distinguished itself clearly from Judaism by its belief in the divinity of Christ. How divine was he? If he was fully divine, were there not two Gods? Or, counting the Holy Spirit, three Gods?

1415

Henry V is on the throne

The Battle of Agincourt is won on Friday 25th October

In the same year, during the Council of Constance, the year of three popes, Jan Hus and one of his supporters, Jerome, were both condemned by the council for heresy. Hus was burnt to death on Saturday 6th of July and Jerome met the same fate on the 30th September. He died in great agony, for he endured the flames much longer than Hus had done, screaming terribly throughout the ordeal. His bones and ashes were broken up and dumped in the Rhine, like those of his friend.

Something of the medieval sense of bloodletting as a remedy for illness seems to have taken hold of the people. The Church as a body was sick; its humours were out of balance. Thus to restore the Church to health, some blood needed to be let. Jerome and Hus would provide that blood.

Ian Mortimer's incredibly well researched book on Henry V and the year 1415 reveal to the modern reader how important religion was to rulers and kings and how necessary it was to them for heresy to be eradicated.

'The huge gathering at Constance may seem to have had little to do with Henry V, who was at Westminster, six hundred miles away. But it mattered a very great deal to him, for five reasons. Sigismund (Holy Roman Emperor) had written to Henry at the start of his reign, asking that he do all he could to work towards the re-unification of the Church. As a religious man, Henry was keen to be involved. He was also no doubt aware that the emperor had written to Henry IV, asking the same thing, and so this represented another opportunity to outdo his father as king. Also, the outcome would be of crucial importance for England, as his learned advisers would have told him. In 1046 a similar confusion of three popes (Gregory VI, Benedict IX and Sylvester III) had been sorted out by the then Holy Roman Emperor at the council of Sutri. The council deposed all three popes and elected a new man in their place. If the council of Constance managed to emulate the council of Sutri, then one man would eventually exercise spiritual authority over the whole of Christendom – and with an exceptionally strong mandate. It would be essential for every Christian king to establish a good relationship with such a man as soon after his election as possible.

The third reason why the council of Constance

was of concern to Henry was the question of what 'reform' of the church would actually involve. Henry had his own programme of religious reform: a list of forty-six points drawn up at his request by the University of Oxford. Among other things, he was concerned with the appointment of bishops, the revocation of illegal appropriations of rectories, the control of lax clergymen who evaded punishment after they had exemption by the pope, and control of the sale of local indulgences. The forth reason for his interest lay in the question of international prestige. Would England be regarded as a nation on its own, alongside France, Italy, Spain and Germany, as it had been at Pisa in 1409? Or would it be subsumed within the mass of 'German' states?

Finally, there was the problem of imposing religious authority, especially with regard to heresy. Jan Hus had been in correspondence with Sir John Oldcastle, Richard Wyche and other English Lollards. Religious thinkers in England continued to circulate the teachings of England's own pre-eminent religious reformer, the late John Wycliffe. Radical ideas such as the pre-eminence of Christ, the unchanged nature of bread and wine in the communion, and the limitations of papal authority were circulated in the form of Wycliffe's writings across the whole of Christendom. And these ideas continued to be hugely divisive, causing fear in those who saw lords, knights and clerics taking them up in Bohemia and Hungary as well as in England. Henry's own confessor, Stephen Patrington – who must have had a spiritual outlook in accord with Henry's own – had bitterly argued against Wycliff at Oxford. The decisions made at Constance concerning Wycliff, Hus and other anti-papal reformers would determine whether Henry was justified in burning such men as heretics, or whether he should tolerate them, and perhaps even listen to them.'

Part 11

The Holy Spirit

Our character and our feelings are often spoken of as our mind or spirit; such as, 'he was a strong-minded person' or 'she was high-spirited.' The Bible uses the words mind and spirit in speaking of our attitude and emotions. When Paul wrote to the Galatians saying, 'The grace of our Lord Jesus Christ be with your spirit, Gal 6:18. He of course was not implying that our spirit is another person connected to us, rather, Paul was referring to our mind, just as when he told the Corinthians that 'I am with you in spirit' he meant his mind was with them, 1Cor 5:4.

In Genesis 41:8, in the NIV, we read of Pharaoh having a troubled mind, yet in the Authorised Version of 1611, it reads, '… his spirit was troubled.' Moving forward to chapter 45:27, we read that Jacob, learning that his son Joseph was alive, 'the spirit of their father Jacob revived,' meaning that what he was told made him feel much better. This connection to our spirit and our mind is reflected in Proverbs 18:14, 'A man's spirit sustains him in sickness, but a crushed spirit who can bear?' This is referring to our strength and weakness in our thinking and our attitude to difficult situations.

Caleb is said to have a different spirit to the other Israelites at that time, Numbers 14:24, that means that his attitude was more wholeheartedly trusting in God than the others.

Jesus said, quoting Deuteronomy 6:5, 'Love the Lord your God with all your heart and with all your soul and with all your mind', Matt 22:37. Our heart, life and mind sums up the totality of who we are, while Ephesians 4:23 speaks of being made new in the attitude of your minds. The 1611 version has, 'And be renewed in the spirit of your mind'. The spirit and attitude of our mind are one and the same; it's our character, our personal identity. Paul spoke of not being conformed any longer to the pattern of this world but be transformed by the renewing of your mind, Rom 12:2.

When Jesus called out, just before his death, with a loud voice, 'Father, into your hands I commit my spirit'. His mind was being placed into God's care, just as Stephen prayed, 'Lord Jesus, receive my spirit'. All that we are, is, in some way, kept in that non-physical part of the brain, called mind, and it will remain safe for the future resurrection of everyone, either the first or the second resurrection.

Our natural mind, what the Bible calls our sinful nature, is hostile to God, making us enemies and alienated from him. Being spiritually dead in our minds toward God, we have become by nature dead, blind and deaf to God through our sins, Eph 2:1,5, Col 2:13, 2 Cor 4:4. The only thing that saves us from God's wrath is God himself. 'Therefore, if anyone is in Christ, the new creation has come: the old has gone, the new is here! All this is from God, who reconciled us to himself through Christ and gave us the ministry of reconciliation: that God was reconciling the world to himself in Christ, not counting people's sins against them' 2 Cor 5:17-19.

Now we come to the point when we can see that God's Spirit is his presence – his mind and character, just as our spirit is our mind and character. How this teaching became the number one doctrine that separated orthodox Christians from heretics will be seen in a later chapter.

William Barclay, in his 'The Plain Man Looks at the Apostle's Creed,' says, It is important and helpful to remember that the word Trinity is not itself a New Testament word. It is even true at least in one sense to say that the doctrine of the Trinity is not directly a New Testament doctrine. It is rather a deduction from, and an interpretation of, the thought and language of the New Testament.

The most important fact of all to remember is that it was not a doctrine which anyone in the church ever sat down and, as it were, worked out from first principles by a series of logical steps; the doctrine of the Trinity has been from the beginning, and must always be seen as, an interpretation of actual Christian experience.'

Anthony Tyrell Hanson, who was the Professor of Theology at the University of Hull, writes, in his book 'The Image of the Invisible God', 'No responsible New Testament scholar would claim that the doctrine of the Trinity was taught by Jesus, or preached by the earliest Christians, or consciously by any writer in the New Testament.'

Bruce Milne, in his book, 'Know the Truth' says, 'just about everything that matters in Christianity hangs on the truth of God's three-in-oneness' he goes on to say, 'the entire fabric of Christian redemption and its application to human experience depend wholly on the three-in-oneness of God. The Trinity is as important as that.' He later gives four texts that imply or state that the Spirit is the third divine person in the Godhead (not a biblical word).

1. Mark 3:29, 'But whoever blasphemes against the Holy Spirit will never be forgiven; he is guilty of an eternal sin.'

2. John 15:26, 'When the counsellor comes, whom I will send to you from the Father, the Spirit of truth who goes out from the Father, he will testify about me.'

3. 1 Cor 6:19, 'Do you not know that your body is a temple of the Holy Spirit, who is in you, whom you have received from God?'

4. 2 Cor 3:17, 'Now the Lord is the Spirit, and where the Spirit of the Lord is, there is freedom.'

Let's take them in order: the context of what Jesus said was in answer to the charge, by the religious leaders that 'he has an evil spirit'. Jesus had been healing all who came to him – people who had an evil spirit, ill with a fever, various diseases, a man who was paralysed, all done because Jesus had compassion on them and for that short period of time the kingdom of God was with them. Peter told the crowd that gathered on the day of Pentecost, 'People of Israel, listen to this: Jesus of Nazareth was a man accredited by God to you by miracles, wonders and signs, which God did among you through him, as you yourselves know', Acts 2:22. These critics of Jesus saw what he was doing and attributed those great signs as being from the devil – their sin will have everlasting consequences.

They had a clear demonstration of God's love in action and said it came from an evil source. They were without excuse.

John 15:26, refers to the gift of God's presence which is promised to all his people and will help them in growing in the grace and knowledge of God.

1 Cor 6:19, another name for God is the Holy Spirit. Jesus said to the woman at the well, 'God is spirit, and his worshippers must worship in spirit and in truth'. It is God within his children that guides and helps us in our weaknesses.

2 Cor 3:17, Yes, the Lord is the Spirit. 'For who has known the mind of the Lord', Paul quotes from Jeremiah, 'that he may instruct him? Paul concludes with, 'But we have the mind of Christ' 1 Cor 2:16. Paul writes in 7:40, 'and I think that I too have the Spirit of God. Having the mind of Christ is the same as having the Spirit of God. Jesus is the embodiment of truth. The truth which the Spirit will disclose is not additional to what Jesus taught, it is a deeper grasp and understanding of that truth.

The gift of the Holy Spirit is pictured as being poured out like water onto believers, Acts 10:45. And at Pentecost it was like fire. Peter said, 'In the last days,' quoting Joel 2, 'I will pour out my Spirit on all people ...' God's Spirit liberates us.

'If anyone loves me, he will obey my teaching. My Father will love him, and we will come to him and make our home with him', John 14:23. This is accomplished through the one Spirit: there is no suggestion of a third person in these texts.

Bruce Milne writes in reference to these four texts, 'The Bible thus presents this unique and mysterious reality: one God, Father, Son and Spirit. A little later, he quotes from the Athanasian Creed, 'We worship one God in Trinity, and Trinity in Unity; neither confounding the Persons: nor dividing the Substance.' There is nothing in the New Testament that that resembles these words; it has all been added since.

The baptism of Jesus is often used in trinitarian teaching to show how the 'three in one' were present at that event. But does it say that, or has that been read into it. John the Baptist should know, as he was there and left a record of what happened from his point of view.

John was told that the one he was waiting for was coming to him, but John did not know how to identify which man it would be so God told him that he would see a sign that would identify the messiah without a shadow of doubt. How about a dove landing on the man and staying on him? That would be as good as a giant arrow pointing directly at him. As John said, 'I would not have known him, except the one who sent me to baptise with water told me, 'the man on whom you see the Spirit come down and remain is the one who will baptise with the Holy Spirit.' After his baptism the dove again came down and a voice from heaven said, 'You are my son, whom I love; with you I am well pleased.'

This dove, representing the Spirit of God, did not come to underline the supposed reality of the trinity, but so that John would know who the Messiah was. He was actually a relative of John. Even when all the biblical texts are examined, such is the devotion of trinitarians, that they will still remain firmly convinced that a teaching only introduced many years after the ink had dried on the last page of the New Testament is clearly taught in the New Testament and suggested in the Old Testament.

The strong and uncompromising statements from Christian leaders, in many books, on the importance of the trinity in Christian theology can be expressed in seven short points.

1. Without a belief in the trinity we could not understand the way of salvation or the gospel.

2. A non-trinitarian God may not be faithful.

3. It is foundational to the church's existence.

4. The early church creeds proclaimed it

5. The Old Testament provides a 'hospitable atmosphere' for the trinity.

6. The reality of God the Father, the Son and the Holy Spirit as triune is the first truth of all mission and the gospel cannot be preached without it.

7. A unity that pleases God is one of belief in the trinity.

Along with the challenges and difficulties that the apostles faced was always the need to be faithful to what Jesus said about himself and his proclamation of the kingdom of God. The trinity was not part of that original teaching, and as such, it was not an issue to defend or promote as the subject of 'the three in one' was not to arise until much later. To say that the gospel could not be preached without it would obviously mean that the apostle's teaching was seriously deficient.

Peter Lewis writes in his 'The Message of the Living God' that the Old Testament provides a 'hospitable atmosphere' for the trinity, yet he quotes Gerald Bray saying 'that we find no clear evidence for such a doctrine in the Old Testament.' The 'hospitable atmosphere' that Peter Lewis speaks of is found, as he says, 'in Jewish thinking in the period between the Testaments'. In other words, in the books not included in either the Old Testament or the New Testament.

'The Bible' writes Michael Ovey, 'stresses God's faithfulness. But faithfulness is possible only within an existing personal relationship. The same arguments apply to faithfulness as they do to love. A non-Trinitarian God means a God for who faithfulness is either irrelevant since he is not personal, or else a God who is finding out about faithfulness as he experiences personal relationships with his creation for the first time. This is devastating since it means that we do not actually know that God is permanently faithful – he might turn out not to be. That doubt eats away at the assurance of our destiny with him', quoted in Peter Lewis's book, p. 288.

This incredible presumption forgets that God was before humans existed and lacked nothing. It attempts to pull God down to our level where we have to learn how to relate through relationships with other people. And through those relationships we learn about doubt and unfaithfulness in ourselves and in others. John wrote that 'we rely on the love

God has for us,' 1 John 4:16, not in the belief of the trinity. The expression 'holy three' as used by Peter Lewis is not biblical. 'We know,' Peter Lewis writes, 'we shall be saved in the hour of death and at the last day because we have been taken up into the company of the *holy three* from whose circle of fellowship none of us will be cast out.'

'Without this truth,' Peter Lewis continues, 'of the Trinitarian being of God our knowledge of the way of salvation in Christ will be impossible. The truth about God as a tri-unity of divine persons is not obfuscation but revelation, clarification and celebration. It is not darkness but light.'

I had listened to a good sermon by John Stott at All Souls, and having read all of his commentaries on books of the New Testament and other very helpful theological books, I decided that I wanted to thank him personally for all that he had written. When I had thanked him and said I was rereading his book on Romans, he asked me how far I had got and I replied, the ninth chapter, and then my mind shut down and I could not think of anything in that chapter or the previous eight chapters, so I thanked him again and walked away thinking I should have had a question prepared.

In John Stott's commentary of Ephesians, p.154, he writes, '… we should all be eager for some visible expression of Christian unity, provided always that we do not sacrifice fundamental truth in order to achieve it. Christian unity arises from our having one Father, one Saviour, and one indwelling Spirit. So we cannot possibly foster a unity which pleases God either if we deny the doctrine of the Trinity or if we have not come personally to know God the Father through the reconciling work of his Son Jesus Christ and by the power of the Holy Spirit.' He also wrote in his commentary on the letters of John, 'The fundamental doctrinal test of the professing Christian concerns his view of the person of Jesus. If he is a Unitarian, or a member of a sect denying the deity of Jesus, he is not a Christian. Many strange cults which have a popular appeal today can be easily judged and quickly repudiated by this test' p.116. *Tyndale New Testament Commentaries.*

If you were to read the greetings at the beginning of each of Paul's letters you will notice that he usually says, 'Grace and peace to you from God our Father and the Lord Jesus Christ'. He never, in that context, mentions the holy spirit sending peace and grace to the readers. In the last verse of 2 Cor 13, Paul writes, 'May the grace of the Lord Jesus Christ, and the love of God, and the fellowship of the Holy Spirit be with you all'. God is spirit and He gives us his spirit to share in his life and in the life to come. Our fellowship is spiritual because of who it comes from. Grace, love and fellowship all come from the same source. 1John 1:3 says, 'and our fellowship is with the Father and with his Son, Jesus Christ,' there is no mention of anyone else.

Paul wrote to the Corinthians in his first letter to them, 'yet for us there is but one God, the Father, from whom all things came and for whom we live; and there is but one Lord, Jesus Christ, through whom all things came and through whom we live', 1Cor 8:6. If Paul believed that the trinity is indispensable to understanding the gospel and receiving salvation, as many Christian leaders tell us, is it not strange that he omitted to mention the holy spirit as a person along with God and the Messiah?

'I charge you,' Paul wrote to Timothy, 'in the sight of God and Christ Jesus and the elect angels …'1Tim 5:21. If the Holy Spirit is a distinct person from the Father and the Son why is he not mentioned before the 'elect angels'?

Calvin's words are often utilised in promoting the trinity. In the paper, Evangelicals Now, July 2009, a full-page article by Oliver Rice begins with 'The theologian of the Holy Spirit' is how B.B. Warfield described John Calvin, whose birth in 1509 we celebrate this year. With Calvin pneumatology (the doctrine of the Holy Spirit) came of age, founded squarely on the Bible.

'I cannot think of the one' Oliver Rice continues, 'without quickly being encircled by the splendour of the three; nor can I discern the three without being straightway carried back to the one.' Words which Calvin quotes from Gregory of Nazianzus and which 'vastly delighted' him, they capture the heart and soul of his theological approach, which is Trinitarian through and through ... Calvin finds the doctrine of the Trinity in the very first chapter of the Bible – in the Spirit hovering over the waters and in the words, 'Let us make ...' Gen 1:26. In the Old Testament overall the doctrine is faintly, but definitely, revealed; in the New, it shines as bright as the noonday sun.

'Trinity is of the very essence of divinity for Calvin. It distinguishes God from all false gods. 'Unless we grasp' quoting Calvin, 'these [three persons in God], only the bare and empty name of God flits about in our brains, to the exclusion of the true God.' When we think of God, or speak or pray, we must think of the triune God.'

Those who believe otherwise are relegated to the theological sidelines as fellowships to be avoided and as having a deadly spiritual contagion. Sensible bible-believing Christians feel secure in standing shoulder to shoulder with other fellowships in condemning all who have a non-trinitarian position.

There was not enough space, or inclination, to include the account of Michael Servetus in Oliver Rice's eulogy of Calvin so Jonathan Wright in his book 'heretics' can fill in the gap.

'Shortly after midday on October 27, 1553, Michael Servetus was marched through the city gates of Geneva, headed for Champel Hill. His heretical meditations on the Trinity had been denounced as 'impious blasphemies and insane errors, wholly foreign to the word of God.' A guard of mounted archers, robed clergymen and magistrates, and much of Geneva's citizenry accompanied the forty-two-year-old Spaniard. They would soon witness one of the sixteenth century's most notorious executions. Servetus was bound to a stake with iron chains, a crown of twigs and sulphur was placed on his head, and sticks of green wood – intended to burn more slowly and thus prolong his suffering – were lit. By some accounts, Servetus let out a cry: '*Misericordia, misericordia.* Jesus have compassion on me.' A copy of his infamous book – *Christianismi Restitutio* (*The Restoration of Christianity*) – burned beneath his feet.

'For more than two decades Michael Servetus had been artfully evading those who sought his downfall. At only twenty years of age he had published a book that launched a theologically confused but full-throated assault on the cherished Christian doctrine of the Trinity. Puzzlingly, Servetus had boldly put his name to this most controversial of tracts (his printer had sensibly remained anonymous), but when inquisitorial proceedings were launched against him, Servetus did not hesitate to adopt a pseudonym. In his new guise as Michel de Villeneuve, he fled to Paris to study mathematics and medicine. A second and third career ensued, in which he served time as a proofreader in Lyon and, with some audacity, worked as the personal physician to the princes of the church (including the archbishop of Vienne) he had so offended.

He remained the theological maverick, however, and in 1545 he made the fateful decision to strike up a correspondence with the great reformer of Geneva, John Calvin. He despised Michael Servetus, and when occasion arose he set out to destroy him. When Servetus's book was published in 1553, the French authorities arrested him and declared him a heretic. It is likely that it was Calvin who informed his Catholic enemies that they had a covert Unitarian in their midst: a curious, some would say disreputable, moment of cross-confessional cooperation in a century of religious strife. Again, however, Servetus made good his escape. Early one morning he scaled the wall of the prison garden in Vienne and headed off to Italy: all that was left to the infuriated French authorities was to burn Servetus in effigy.

Bizarrely, and catastrophically, Servetus decided to stop off at Geneva on route. (in Andrew Atherstone's account in *'The Reformation: Faith & Flames* he writes, 'Servetus began a lengthy correspondence with Calvin and sent him a copy of his manuscript, but the reformer rejected these ideas as 'wild imaginings'. When the Spaniard proposed a visit to Geneva in 1547, Calvin told Farel: 'I am unwilling to guarantee his safety, for if he does come and my authority counts for anything, I will never let him get away alive.'

Servetus had arrived on a Sunday and took the risky step of going to see John Calvin preach in one of the cities churches. Calvin, out of theological distaste and in order to reassert his waning political influence, engineered Servetus's arrest and trial. A boisterous examination of Servetus's opinions followed, in which the heretic was charged with spreading 'endless blasphemies,' calling the baptism of children 'an invention of the devil,' and even studying the detested Koran 'in order to controvert and disprove the doctrine and religion that the Christian churches hold.' Worst of all, he had allegedly described the Trinity as a 'three-headed devil, like to Cerberus, whom the ancient poets have called the dog of hell, a monster.'

Servetus's guilt was established to the satisfaction of the city's Lesser Council and while Geneva sought the advice of other Swiss cities about how best to proceed, Servetus languished in prison. He complained endlessly about his plight. 'The lice eat me alive.' He informed the city's magistrates, 'my clothes are torn, and I have nothing for a change, neither a jacket nor a shirt'; realizing that his prospects were bleak, he pleaded that he might be killed in a humane a way as possible. It was commonly supposed that the true martyr would endure his final agonies with unworldly serenity. Servetus feared that, if the flames began to lick, he would respond with a distinct lack of courage. As we have seen, his requests fell on deaf ears.

The context of Servetus's execution is all important. By 1553, the rigors of John Calvin's regime were already known. Nowhere was the concept of a controlled, magisterial Reformation more in evidence. During the 1540s and 1550s, as much as 7% of Geneva's population was brought before its ecclesiastic tribunal, the Consistory: Protestant's very own Inquisition. Some offenders had done nothing more heinous than play cards or don extravagant clothes. Others were adulterers, blasphemers, and religious dissidents, many of whom received punishments – ranging from excommunication, to banishment, to execution – that even by the standards of the sixteenth century were unusually severe. It was all part of Calvin's plan to reform the morality of the city he hoped to turn into a Protestant paradise. Pierre Ameaux criticized Calvin's penchant for employing French preachers in Geneva's churches. As punishment, he was made to parade through the city's streets in a hair shirt, begging for forgiveness. Valentin Gentilis held theological views that Calvin found unagreeable, and was made to undergo the humiliation of publicly burning his own books. And yet, even in this oppressive climate, the particularly gruesome death of Michael Servetus stands out.

One contemporary, the French theologian Sebastian Castellio, 1515- 1563, found the whole episode deeply shameful. For Castellio, the execution was an unforgivable act of tyranny. He began to wonder if the very notion of persecuting heretics was not a betrayal of the entire Christian cause. Just what were heretics, Castellio asked:

simply those with whom we disagree. And while you might detest the people with whom you quarrelled, it really wasn't appropriate to torture and kill them. Force and violence had no role to play in the arena of religious belief because the truth could not be hammered into people's minds. Persuasion was endlessly more efficient than coercion.

Castellio asked his Christ a rhetorical question, 'I beg you in the name of your Father, do you now command that those who do not understand your precepts, be drowned in water, cut with lashes to the entrails, dismembered by the sword, or burned at a slow fire? Did Christ approve of these things being done in his name? Are they your vicars who make these sacrifices? Of course not. O blasphemous and shameful audacity of men, who dare to attribute to Christ that which they do by the command and the instigation of Satan.'

Those who teach and believe in the trinity have too much invested to contemplate change. The best response, in their minds, is to attack those who dare challenge it, or gently take the person to one side and explain the scriptures by careful editing and selection of just those portions they think back up their position. Most of what they would claim as evidence for the trinity is read back into the text rather than read out of it. Even Genesis 1:26 is held up as teaching the trinity, 'Let *us* make man in our image …' There you are, three, they will tell you, when the word 'us' just means more than one. Putting three in place of 'us' is not good hermeneutics or correct exegesis.

A question that needs to be asked is who was involved in the introduction of the trinity teaching, and can we discover when and over what period of time did this teaching become established?

Part 12

Who & When

Athenagoras was a Christian apologist and philosopher from Athens. Around 177 he presented the emperor Marcus Aurelius and his son, Commodus, with a work entitled *Plea for the Christians*. This was a work from a philosopher to rulers who were themselves philosophers. Its aim was to counter charges against the Christians and to say that Christianity was compatible with the best Greek philosophy. He said that 'reason demonstrates that there is one God, the creator of all things, who is transcendent, eternal, and incomprehensible. But Christians are also able to affirm these things in what the Scriptures say, where the witness of the prophets testifies to the character of God as triune.' This is possible the earliest reference to God as triune.

Irenaeus (140-200) taught that there is one God who creates and saves. There can be no question of creation being the work of a lessor deity. God always has with him his Word and his Spirit, pictured by

Irenaeus as God's 'two hands'. His conception of God was trinitarian.

Hippolytus (170-236) was an elder in the Roman church and was the last significant figure in the Western church to write in Greek. Hippolytus argued that there is one God but it was necessary to distinguish between the Father, the Son and the Holy Spirit. The three were distinct *prosopa*, or 'persons'. His way of establishing the distinctions between these 'persons' was not very successful. He claimed that the *Logos became* the Son in the incarnation, and thus the term *Son* should only be used of the incarnate Christ, not the pre-existent Lord; in effect, Jesus Christ was only a creature to whom divinity had been assigned for the duration of his saving ministry. The Holy Spirit was in practice not all that significant, either. As was the case in much of the theology of the second and early third centuries. Most of the attention in Hippolytus's reflection on the nature of God was focused on the Father-Son relationship.

Tertullian (160-225) was the first Christian writer of any importance to express himself in Latin. Like Irenaeus, he insists that creation and redemption are the work of one God, but he is equally insistent that this God carries out his will in a three-fold manner, acting simultaneously as the Father, the Son, and the Holy Spirit. For him, threeness and oneness are not, in God, mutually exclusive.

There is, he says, one divine *substantia*, 'substance,' within the three *personae*, 'persons,' and the nature of God is best described by the word *Trinitas*, 'Trinity.' This word was used first by Tertullian. It translated a Greek word with the same sense, *trias*, 'threeness,' used already of God by the apologist Athenagoras. Tertullian furnished Trinitarian doctrine with the technical vocabulary that would be used from that time on by the majority of Christians.

Unity of Christian belief was of colossal importance. In the interests of preserving the social and political stability of the emperor's dominions, it was now his duty to stamp out any divisions and dissensions within the Christian community. Heterodoxy (not following the usual or accepted standards or beliefs) was now a political challenge, and a heretic was comparable to a traitor. Deviance from orthodoxy was now a crime. As Constantine had informed his empire, heretics were to be treated as the pests of society and the pernicious enemies of the human race.

Such thoughts would gather considerable pace in the century after Constantine, and no document sums up the new political ramifications of heresy quite as well as the rewriting of Roman law given by the emperor Justinian between 529 and 534, which were issued in the joint names of Lord Jesus Christ and the emperor himself. All citizens were to come forward for Christian baptism, 'Should they disobey, let them know that they will be excluded from the state and will no longer have any right of possession, neither goods or property; stripped of everything, they will be reduced to penury, without prejudice to the appropriate punishments that will be imposed on them.'

An article in a Christian magazine by Guy A. Davis has the following, 'Evangelism in its best and most consistent form is an expression of the Reformed faith. And it is worth stressing that the reformers had no wish to reject the theological heritage of the church and start again from scratch. They saw themselves as defenders of the catholic tradition that had been corrupted by the Roman Catholic Church of their day. The reformers held to the ancient Trinitarian creeds and the teachings of the church fathers, especially Augustine, with his emphasis on the sovereignty of grace. Of course, they taught that the Holy Spirit speaking in scripture is the supreme authority, but they were catholic in outlook, holding to the faith confessed by the church throughout the ages.'

Eamon Duffy makes the point in his 'Fires of Faith: Catholic England under Mary Tudor', 'If protestant defiance had provided the trigger for the regime's resort to force, no one could seriously have doubted the inevitability of such an outcome. Some protestants, including several future victims of the burnings, would challenge the very idea that a government should 'in a matter of faith use compulsion, nor violence, because faith is a gift of God, and cometh not of man, neither of man's laws, neither at such time as men require it'. Both the layman Thomas Haukes and the cleric John Bradford would challenge Bishop Bonner in almost identical words: 'where prove you that Christ or his apostles killed any man for his faith?' Such opinions are hardly surprising from the mouths of men facing execution for their beliefs. In fact, however, most protestant leaders agreed with their catholic counterparts that false faith was worse than no faith at all, and that those stubbornly adhering to religious error were rightly condemned to death.' Both sides supported the death penalty for going against orthodoxy.

There was a strong move against Catholics during the reign of Elizabeth I. In 1585 a new bill was introduced in parliament and the historian Jessie Childs fills in the details in her book 'God's Traitors *Terror & Faith in Elizabethan England*'. 'The bill was 'against Jesuits, Seminary Priests and such other like disobedient persons. It was designed to annihilate the English mission. Any priest ordained abroad since the accession of the Queen and found in England after forty days of promulgation would automatically be deemed a traitor and face the death penalty. Anyone who wittingly harboured him would be judged as a 'felon' and suffer 'death, loss and forfeit as in case of one attained of felony'. The bill presented an impossible scenario for England's Catholics. Their one hope lay with Queen Elizabeth, 'our headspring and fountain of mercy'. In a long petition they begged for a measure of toleration. 'O most lamentable condition,' they cried:

If we receive them (by whom we know no evil at all) it shall be deemed treason in us. If we shut our doors and deny our temporal relief to our Catholic pastors in respect of their function, then are we already judged most damnable traitors to Almighty God ... Albeit that many ways we have been afflicted, yet this affliction following (if it be not by the accustomed natural benignity of your Majesty suspended or taken away) will light upon us to our extreme ruin and certain calamity: that either we (being Catholics) must live as bodies without souls, or else lose the temporal use both of body and soul.

'Suffer us not,' they begged the Queen, 'to be the only outcasts and refuse of the world':

Let not us, your Catholic native English and obedient subjects, stand in more peril for frequenting the Blessed Sacraments and exercising the Catholic religion (and that most secretly) than do the Catholic subjects to the Turk publicly, than do the perverse and blasphemous Jews haunting their synagogue under sundry Christian kings openly, and than do the Protestants enjoying their public assemblies under diverse Catholic kings and princes quietly. Let it not be treason for the sick man in body (even at the last gasp) to seek ghostly counsel for the salvation of his soul of a Catholic priest.

One of the petitioners, Richard Shelley, put the document in the Queen's hands as she took the air in Greenwich Park. His presumption was rewarded with a cell in Marshalsea prison … while the petitioners' first allegiance was to God – a Catholic God who, through the Pope, had excommunicated Elizabeth I – their love, loyalty and duty to the heretic Queen would always be qualified. Burghley's confidant, Robert Beale, had expressed his concern earlier: 'It is impossible that they should love her, whose religion founded in the Pope's authority maketh her birth and title unlawful.'

And yet so many of them did love her – despite the bull of excommunication and despite the repressive laws … Many Catholics would have loved nothing more than to have been a good Englishman and a good Catholic. Parliament and the papacy conspired to make it impossible.'

Kegan A. Chandler quotes professor Jason D. BeDuhn in his book 'The God of Jesus In Light of Christian Dogma', 'When the Protestant Reformation occurred just five hundred years ago, it did not reinvent Christianity from scratch, but carried over many of the doctrines that had developed within Catholicism over the course of the previous thousand years and more. In this sense, one might argue that the Protestant Reformation is incomplete, that it did not fully realize the high ideals that were set for it.' *Truth in Translation*.

Edward Gibbon perceptibly notes that 'the reformers were ambitious of succeeding tyrants whom they had dethroned. They imposed with equal rigor their creeds and confessions; They asserted the right of the magistrate to punish heretics with death. The nature of the tiger was the same.'

Church history Meic Pearse, in his introduction to 'The Great Restoration: The religious radicals of the 16th and 17th centuries' writes, concerning Christianity, 'It did not seek to convert governments but people; it did not focus on public rituals but on the attitude of the heart. One entered such a church by personal regeneration. Yet by the Middle Ages – and the effects have continued into the modern world – this church had become a monster, claiming universal authority over human society. Its infinitely numerous rules and regulations affected every part of political and social life, and participation of the whole population was compulsory. Deviations from its orthodoxy (which in any case differed from the orthodoxy of the early church) was, moreover, punishable by death at the stake.

'Christianity and Judaism had thus traded places … The infant church had suffered persecution from the synagogues; medieval Christendom persecuted the Jews with a savagery that was not abated by the Reformation, and the pogroms have continued down to modern times.'

The safest place for a Christian to live during the 16th century was Transylvania. Diarmaid MacCulloch writes in his book, 'Writings on the Reformation', 'It is sad that we remember the former eastern European principality of Transylvania for Count Dracula, who never existed, rather than as the first Christian polity officially to declare that everyone ought to be able to worship God in their own way without interference. The Transylvania Diet (that is, its Parliament) spelled this out as early as 1568, in a declaration made in the parish church of a town called Torda, a place which should be more of a centre of pilgrimage than it is:

Ministers should everywhere preach and proclaim [the Gospel] according to their understanding of it, and if their community is willing to accept this, good; if not, however; no one should be compelled by force if their spirit is not at peace, but a minister retained whose teaching is pleasing to the community ... no one is permitted to threaten to imprison or banish anyone because of their teaching, because faith is a gift from God.

The French artist James Tissot (1863-1902) painted and drew hundreds of illustrations for his two volumes of 'The Life of Christ', in both Latin and English. These two large books, printed in

Paris were kindly given to me by my mother-in-law Joan. In his introduction he wrote, 'For a long time the imagination of the Christian world has been led astray by the fancies of artists; there is a whole army of delusions to be overturned before any ideas can be entertained approaching the truth in the slightest degree.'

Most of us are taught, through paintings and films, that the crucifixion of Jesus was on a hill, remember the hymn 'There is a green hill far away' which I used to sing at school in Barry. Yet the gospels are silent regarding any hill at the execution site. The Romans, who used that dreadful slow method of killing people would always position the crosses at a place the public would find difficult to avoid, although public executions inevitably drew many people to witness these gory events, as they have always done. A busy road or a central meeting place would do. Just outside one of Jerusalem's main gates would serve this dark purpose as many would be going in and out of the gates as well as travelling north or south to the next gate.

We have mental images from so many films of Jesus himself that it's very difficult to erase them when we read from the biblical accounts the things he did. Film music helps make the visuals so much more moving and dramatic as Miklos Rozsa did for

Ben Hur and King of Kings. In the pre-crucifixion scene we see the other condemned men carrying the cross beam which is factual but Jesus is seen in both of these films, and the others, carrying the whole cross. Why? Because that is the way it has been depicted in all the paintings going back centuries. For many people that's as much theology they get. Jesus' cross would not have been different from the other condemned men that day.

When a child is born arrangements are usually made for the baby to be baptised because that's what is expected and if you didn't you might be called an atheist or heretic even. Very few would seek any biblical ground for this event and some ministers or priests might tell you that Jesus said, 'Let the little children come to me, and do not hinder them, for the kingdom of heaven belongs to such as these.' While leaving out the part when Jesus placed his hands on the children and blessed them. It should be noted that in Matthew's account that he is addressing primarily a Jewish audience who would be sensitive to the use of the word God, as some are today. So while the other gospel writers speak of 'the kingdom of God' Matthew replaces the word 'God' with the more acceptable word, 'heaven'.

While people are free today to baptise their

baby or not, it was very different in the 1500s when Anabaptists were put to death for rejecting child baptism, saying that a person needs to come to faith and repentance first before being baptised. Martin Luther condemned their teachings.

Augustine of Hippo explicitly defended God's justice in sending newborn and stillborn babies to hell if they died without baptism.

In Jon Meacham's biography of Thomas Jefferson, we read on pages 122-123, 'In his *Notes on the State of Virginia*, a book written a few years after his service revising the laws in the General Assembly, Jefferson was honest about his state's abysmal record on liberty of conscience. It was a crime in Virginia not to baptise infants in the Anglican church; dissenters were denied office, civil or military; children could be taken from their parents if the parents failed to profess the proscribed creeds … He said such a system led to 'spiritual tyranny.' In theological terms, according to notes he made on John Locke, Jefferson concurred with a Christian tradition that held the church should not depend on state-enforced compulsion. Summarising Locke, Jefferson wrote that 'our Saviour chose not to propagate his religion by temporal punishments or civil incapacitation'; had Jesus chosen to do so, 'it was in his almighty power' to force belief. Instead, 'he chose to … extend it by its influence on reason, thereby showing to others how [they] should proceed.'

Part 13

Herod Agrippa II

Jesus was talking to his disciples about what would be happening before his return and said, 'Nation will rise against nation, and kingdom against kingdom. There will be great earthquakes, famines and pestilences in various places, and fearful events and great signs from heaven. But before all this, they will lay hands on you and persecute you. They will deliver you to synagogues and prisons, and you will be brought before kings and governors, and all on account of my name ... Luke 21:10-12.

The apostle Paul was brought before King Agrippa and Luke gives us a detailed account of what he said. But before we read that the late John Stott can introduce us to important information leading up to Paul's explanation of why he came to be standing before a king.

On page 358 of Stott's commentary on the book of Acts, 1991, he writes, 'Jerusalem and Rome were the centres of two enormously strong power blocks. The faith of Jerusalem went back two millennia to

Abraham. The rule of Rome extended some three million square miles round the Mediterranean Sea. Jerusalem's strength lay in history and tradition, Rome's in conquest and organisation. The combined might of Jerusalem and Rome was overwhelming. If a solitary dissident like Paul were to set himself against them, the outcome would be inevitable. His chances of survival would resemble those of a butterfly before a steamroller. He would be crushed, utterly obliterated from the face of the earth.

Yet such an outcome, we may confidently affirm, never even entered Paul's mind as a possibility. For he saw his situation from an entirely different perspective. He was no traitor to either church or state, that he should come into collision with them, although this is how his accusers tried to frame him. The enemies of Jesus had followed the same ploy. In their own court they had accused him of threatening to destroy the temple and of blaspheming while before Pilate they had represented him as guilty of sedition – subverting the nation, opposing taxes to Caesar and claiming to be himself a king. Now Paul's enemies laid similar charges against him, namely that he had offended against the law of the Jews, against the temple and against Caesar.

But Paul was as innocent in these areas as Jesus had been. He had no quarrel with the God-given status of either Rome or Jerusalem. On the contrary, as he had written to the Roman Christians, he recognised that the authority given to Rome came from God and that the privileges given to Israel came from God also. The gospel did not undermine the law, whether Jewish or Roman, but rather upheld it. To be sure, The Romans might misuse their God-given authority and the Jews might misrepresent their law as the means of salvation. In such situations Paul would oppose them. But that was not the issue now. Paul's contention, while on trial, was that in principle the gospel both supports the rule of Caesar and fulfils the hope of Israel. His defence before his judges was to present himself as a loyal citizen of Rome and a loyal son of Israel.'

Ten pages later, after dealing with Paul's appearances before the governors Felix and Festus, Stott gives us a short biography of Agrippa. 'Herod Agrippa II was the son of Herod Agrippa I of Acts 12 and the great grandson of Herod the Great. Bernice was his sister, and rumours were rife that their relationship was incestuous. Because he had been only seventeen years old when his father died, he was considered too young to assume the kingdom of Judea, which therefore reverted to rule by procurator, he was given a tiny and insignificant northern kingdom within what is now Lebanon, and this was later augmented by territory in Galilee. He was nevertheless influential in Jewry because the emperor Claudius had committed to him both the care of the temple and the appointment of the high priest. He and Bernice came to Caesarea to pay their respects to the new procurator, and during their stay Festus raised Paul's case, which he had inherited from Felix.'

Now we come to Paul's appearing before Agrippa.

'Then Agrippa said to Paul, 'you have permission to speak for yourself.'

So Paul motioned with his hand and began his defence: 'King Agrippa, I consider myself fortunate to stand before you today as I make my defence against all the accusations of the Jews, and especially so because you are well acquainted with all the Jewish customs and controversies. Therefore, I beg you to listen to me patiently.

'The Jewish people all know the way I have lived ever since I was a child, from the beginning of my life in my own country, and also in Jerusalem. They have known me for a long time and can testify, if they are willing, that I conformed to the strictest sect of our religion, living as a Pharisee. And now it is because of my hope in what God has promised our ancestors that I am on trial today. This is the promise our twelve tribes are hoping to see fulfilled as they earnestly serve God day and night. King Agrippa, it is because of this hope that the Jews are accusing me. Why should any of you consider it incredible that God raises the dead?

'I too was convinced that I ought to do all that was possible to oppose the name of Jesus of Nazareth. And that is just what I did in Jerusalem. On the authority of the chief priests I put many of the Lord's people in prison, and when they were put to death, I cast my vote against them. Many a time I went from one synagogue to another to have them punished, and I tried to force them to blaspheme. I was so obsessed with persecuting them that I even hunted them down in foreign cities.

'On one of these journeys I was going to Damascus with the authority and commission of the chief priests. About noon, King Agrippa, as I was on the road, I saw a light from heaven, brighter than the sun, blazing around me and my companions. We all fell to the ground, and I heard a voice saying to me in Aramaic, 'Saul, Saul, why do you persecute me? It is hard for you to kick against the goads' (or as Eugine H. Peterson has, 'why do you insist on going against the grain?).

'Then I asked, 'Who are you Lord?'

'I am Jesus, whom you are persecuting,' the Lord replied. 'Now get up and stand on your feet. I have appeared to you to appoint you as a servant and as a witness of what you have seen and will see of me. I will rescue you from your own people and from the Gentiles. I am sending you to them to open their eyes and turn them from darkness to light, and from the power of Satan to God, so that they may receive forgiveness of sins and a place among those who are sanctified by faith in me.'

'So then, King Agrippa, I was not disobedient to the vision from heaven. First to those in Damascus, then to those in Jerusalem and in all Judea, and then to the Gentiles, I preached that they should repent and turn to God and demonstrate their repentance by their deeds. That is why some Jews seized me in the temple courts and tried to kill me. But God has helped me to this very day; so I stand here and testify to small and great alike. I am saying nothing beyond what the prophets and Moses said would happen – that the Messiah would suffer and, as the first to rise from the dead, would bring the message of light to his own people and to the Gentiles.'

At this point Festus interrupted Paul's defence. 'You are out of your mind, Paul' he shouted. 'Your great learning is driving you insane.'

'I am not insane, most excellent Festus,' Paul

replied. 'What I am saying is true and reasonable. The King is familiar with these things, and I can speak freely to him. I am convinced that none of this has escaped his notice, because it was not done in a corner. King Agrippa, do you believe the prophets? I know you do.'

Then Agrippa said to Paul, 'Do you think that in such a short time you can persuade me to be a Christian?'

Paul replied, 'Short time or long – I pray to God that not only you but all who are listening to me today may become what I am, except for these chains.'

The king rose, and with him the governor and Bernice and those sitting with them. After they left the room, they began saying to one another, 'This man is not doing anything that deserves death or imprisonment.'

Agrippa said to Festus, 'This man could have been set free if he had not appealed to Caesar.'

Acts 26

Paul said, in this inspired speech, what happens to a person if they repent and turn to God. What they receive stands in contrast to how we all are before coming to God in repentance: Our eyes were closed, we were blind, now they are open, we were living in darkness, now we are living in the light, now we can see, we were in the power of Satan, the god of this world, now we belong to God, our Father. We now have been forgiven and set apart, along with many others, by trust and belief in the Messiah Jesus.

Part 14

War

Ernie Pyle was unique as a war correspondent. Only rarely did he write about the so-called big picture, the involved strategies concocted by military brass. Rather, Pyle focused on the individual combatant – on how he lived, endured by turns battle and boredom, and sometimes on how he died, far from home in a war whose origins he only vaguely understood.

In North Africa, Sicily, Italy, France, and in the Pacific, Ernie Pyle lived with the men he wrote about, six times weekly offering thirteen million stateside readers his 'worm's-eye-view' of what it was like for the American fighting in the biggest war ever.

But Pyle's work provided much more than a wealth of documentary detail about the World War II era's hero, the citizen soldier. Pyle also explained (and decried) the moral changes the war forced upon its participants, the rapid conversion of the boy next door into a trained and enthusiastic killer.

When Pyle was killed by a Japanese sniper's machine-gun bullet on the tiny Island of Ie Shima in the spring of 1945, for everyone – President Truman, those on the home front, and GIs the world over – the outpouring of grief was both genuine and effusive.

From the inside flap of 'Ernie's War' by David Nichols

The following is a rough draft of a column Pyle had been preparing for release upon the end of the war in Europe. It was found on his body the day he was killed on Ie Shima, twenty days before the Germans surrendered.

'On Victory in Europe

And so it is over. The catastrophe on one side of the world has run its course. The day that it had so long seemed would never come has come at last.

I suppose that emotions here in the Pacific are the same as they were among the allies all over the world. First a shouting of the good news with such joyous surprise that you would think the shouter himself had brought it about.

And then an unspoken sense of gigantic

relief – and then a hope that the collapse in Europe would hasten the end in the Pacific.

It has been seven months since I heard my last shot in the European war. Now I am as far away from it as it is possible to get on this globe.

This is written on a little ship lying off the coast of the Island of Okinawa, just south of Japan, on the other side of the world from Ardennes.

But my heart is still in Europe, and that's why I am writing this column.

It is to the boys who were my friends for so long. My one regret of the war is that I was not with them when it ended.

For the companionship of two and a half years of death and misery is a spouse that tolerates no divorce. Such companionship finally becomes part of one's soul, and it cannot be obliterated.

True, I am with American boys in the other war not yet ended, but I am old-fashioned and my sentiment runs to old things.

To me the European war is old, and the Pacific war is new.

Last summer I wrote that I hoped the end of the war could be a gigantic relief, but not an elation. In the joyousness of high spirits it is easy for us to forget the dead. Those who are gone would not wish themselves to be a millstone of gloom around our necks.

But there are many of the living who have had burned into their brains forever the unnatural sight of cold dead men scattered over the hillsides and in the ditches along the high rows of hedge throughout the world.

Dead men by mass production – in one country after another – month after month and year after year. Dead men in winter and dead men in summer.

Dead men in such familiar promiscuity that they become monotonous.

Dead men in such monstrous infinity that you come almost to hate them.

These are the things that you at home need not even try to understand. To you at home they are columns of figures, or he is a near one who went away and just didn't come back. You didn't see him lying so grotesque and pasty beside the gravel road in France.

We saw him, saw him by the multiple thousands. That's the difference …'

Ernie Pyle

Whatever day you are reading this there are people dying in wars. Winston S. Churchill wrote an article that was published in 1925 and later incorporated into his book 'Thoughts and Adventures' in 1932. I have the 1943 edition. One of his chapters is titled 'Shall we all commit suicide?' and he writes of new weapons that are being planned or imagined that could wipe out whole cities. He begins his essay with these words:

'The story of the human race is War. Except for brief and precarious interludes, there has never been peace in the world; and before history began, murderous strife was universal and unending.'

There have been many wars that we do not know about as records were not kept or have been lost. The Bible gives accounts of many conflicts that otherwise we would not know of. At the time of Noah we read that 'the earth was corrupt in God's sight and was full of violence.' Some could say that nothing has changed in that regard.

TO THE READER

From the beginning of Peter Englund's 2011 book 'The Beauty and the Sorrow'

The famous American war correspondent Stanley Washburn was invited in 1915 to contribute to *The Times History of the War*. He refused, even though he had been asked by none other than the mighty Lord Northcliffe: 'I told him quite frankly that I did not want to write anything during the war which was published under the name of "history", saying that, in my opinion, no one who lived in a campaign could possibly be sufficiently well informed, nor have the proper perspective, to write anything of that nature.'

I have had reason to think of Washburn's words on a number of occasions. I am an academic historian by profession but I have also tried my hand as a war correspondent in the Balkans, in Afghanistan and, most recently, in Iraq. As a historian, there have been many times when I have longed to be present where and when events happen, but once I arrived in, say, Kabul, I discovered the same thing as many other people in the same situations: to be right in the middle of events is no guarantee of being able to understand them. You are stuck in a confusing, chaotic and noisy reality and the chances are that the editorial office on the other side of the planet often has a better idea of what is going on than you do …'

The Bible gives us that perspective that we in the mess of life are unable to see. It reveals what the human eye cannot see and it is only that written source that can give us the understanding of what is really happening.

In the book of Revelation, where we earlier saw in chapter 12, of the woman giving birth to a son and the dragon standing in front of the woman to kill her child the moment he was born, then, a few verses later, we read, 'And there was war in heaven. Michael and his angels fought against the dragon, and the dragon and his angels fought back. But he was not strong enough, and they lost their place in heaven. The great dragon was hurled down – that ancient snake called the devil, or Satan, who leads the whole world astray. He is hurled to the earth, and his angels with him … He is filled with fury, because he knows that his time is short … the dragon was enraged at the woman and went off to make war against the rest of her offspring – those who keep God's commands and hold fast their testimony about Jesus, Rev 12:7-9, 12b, 17.

There are wars that are seen and experienced but there are also wars that are real but not seen. There is also the inner conflict between our sinful nature and God's Holy Spirit. Paul writes to the Galatians, 'So I say, live by the Spirit, and you will not gratify the desires of the sinful nature. For the sinful nature desires what is contrary to the Spirit, and the Spirit what is contrary to the sinful nature. They are in conflict, or as the NRSV has, for these are opposed to each other, to prevent you from doing what you want. But if you are led by the Spirit, you are not subject to the law, Gal 5:17-18. Paul expressed this spiritual battle to the Romans, 'we know that the law is spiritual; but I am unspiritual, sold as a slave to sin. I don't understand what I do. For what I want to do I don't do, but what I hate I do. And if I do what I don't want to do, I agree that the law is good. As it is, It is no longer I myself who do it, but it is the sin living in me … for I have the desire to do what is good, but I can't carry it out … in my inner being I delight in God's law, but I see another law at work in me, waging war against the law of my mind and making me a prisoner of the law of sin at work within me … The sinful mind is hostile to God; it doesn't submit to God's law, nor can it do so. Those controlled by the sinful nature cannot please God, Rom 7: 14-23, 8: 7-8.

As well as recording numerous wars, the Bible speaks of a time when there will be no wars, as already quoted on page 54, 'Many nations will come and say, Come, let us go up to the mountain of the Lord, to the house of the God of Jacob. He will teach us his ways, so that we may walk in his paths. The law will go out from Zion, the word of the Lord from Jerusalem.

He will judge between many peoples and will settle disputes for strong nations far and wide. They will beat their swords into ploughshares and their spears into pruning hooks. Nation will not take up sword against nation, nor will they train for war any more' Micah 4:2-3, about 700 B.C.

But what about the Christian now? With inner conflicts and battles that spring from our own human nature, and attacks from outside that are out of our control. How do we fight an enemy that we cannot see? An enemy that wants to destroy us.

'Finally, be strong in the Lord and in his mighty power. Put on the full armour of God, so you can take your stand against the devil's schemes. For our struggle is not against flesh and blood, but against the rulers, against the authorities, against the powers of this dark world and against the spiritual forces of evil in the heavenly realms. Therefore put on the full armour of God, so that when the day of evil comes, you may be able to stand your ground, and after you have done everything, to stand' Eph 6:10-13.

James adds, 'Submit yourselves to God. Resist the devil, and he will flee from you. Come near to God and he will come near to you', and Peter also writes, 'Be alert and of sober mind. Your enemy the devil prowls around like a roaring lion looking for someone to devour. Resist him, standing firm in the faith, because you know that your fellow-believers throughout the world are undergoing the same kind of sufferings', James 4:7-8. 1Peter 5:8-9.

Part 15

Listen

As we read, on page 147, the emperor Justinian made life very difficult for those who did not want to become Christians as he wanted all people – the whole empire, to believe in the same things or else. Meic Pearse says in his book 'The Gods of War' 'Nations cannot be Christian; only individuals can. If Christians can fight, then it cannot be for Christianity, for that is a contradiction of Christ himself'.

Justinian also went after the Jews by his new law *Servitus Judaeorum* (Servitude of the Jews) 530 AD. Jews and other no-Christians were denied citizenship and conversion to Judaism became a capital offence, as did the ownership of Christian slaves by Jews. Hebrew payer was banned as well as the recitation of the *Shema* which was condemned as being anti-trinitarian.

The *Shema* was a statement of faith that was repeated every day by religious Jews. *Shema* is the Hebrew for 'hear' or 'listen', and comes from Deuteronomy 6:4.

One of the teachers of the law came and heard them debating. Noticing that Jesus had given them a good answer, he asked him, 'Of all the commandments, which is the most important?

'The most important one,' answered Jesus, 'is this: 'Hear O Israel: the Lord our God, the Lord is one. Love the Lord your God with all your heart and with all your soul and with all your mind and with all your strength.' The second is this: 'Love your neighbour as yourself.' There is no commandment greater than these.'

'Well said, teacher,' the man replied. 'You are right in saying that God is one and there is no other but him …'

Mark 12:28-32

The biblical teaching that God is one is held by trinitarians as encompassing the three persons in one. Now we will look at other texts regarding what some of the prophets wrote and what Jesus said, as well as what the apostles said and wrote.

Isa 44:6 This is what the Lord says – Israel's King and Redeemer, the Lord Almighty: I am the first and the last; apart from me there is no God.

Micah 5:4 He will stand and shepherd his flock in the strength of the Lord, in the majesty of the name the Lord his God. And they will live securely, for then his greatness will reach to the ends of the earth.

John 17:3 Now this is eternal life: that they may know you, the only true God, and Jesus Christ, whom you have sent.

John 20:17 I am ascending to my Father and your Father, to my God and your God.

Rev 3:12 I will write on them the name of my God and the city of my God.

Rev 1: 5-6 … Jesus Christ, who is the faithful witness, the firstborn from the dead, and the ruler of the kings of the earth. To him who loves us and has freed us from our sins by his blood, and has made us to be a kingdom and priests to serve his God and Father …

1Tim 2:5 For there is one God and one mediator between God and human beings, Christ Jesus.

Acts 2:22 People of Israel, listen to this: Jesus of Nazareth was a man accredited by God to you by miracles, wonders and signs, which God did among you through him, as you yourselves know.

John 8:40 you are looking for a way to kill me, a man who has told you the truth that I heard from God.

Acts 17:31 For he has set a day when he will judge the world with justice by the man he has appointed.

Rom 5:15 … for if the many died by the trespass of the one man, how much more did God's grace and the gift that came by the grace of the one man, Jesus Christ, overflow to the many.

1Cor 15:21 For since death came through a human being, the resurrection of the dead comes also through a human being.

1Cor 15:45 So it is written, the first Adam became a living being, the last Adam, a life-giving spirit.

Rom 15:6 so that with one mind and one voice you may glorify the God and Father of our Lord Jesus Christ.

1Peter 1:3 Praise be to the God and Father of our Lord Jesus Christ.

Heb 1:9 You have loved righteousness and hated wickedness, therefore God, your God, has set you above your companions.

Eph 4:6 One God and Father of all.

Eph 1:17 I keep asking that the God of our Lord Jesus Christ, the glorious Father, may give you the spirit of wisdom and revelation.

Matt 27:46 … My God, my God, why have you forsaken me?

Rev 22:16 I, Jesus, have sent my angel to give you this testimony for the churches. I am the root and the offspring of David, and the bright morning star.

When Peter had finished speaking to the people on that day of Pentecost about three thousand of them were baptised and added to the church. Earlier we read that, according to Trinitarians, the true gospel cannot be preached without the teaching of the Trinity. Peter called Jesus, 'a man accredited by God' and without any hint whatsoever of God in three persons, so were those conversions that special day invalid?

In Matthews account Jesus was descended from Abraham and in Luke's account he traces the line all the way back to Adam, the son of God. Both state that Jesus was a descendent of David. He belonged to the house and line of David and was promised the throne of his father David and that he would reign over the house of Jacob for ever; his kingdom would never end. He was given the name Joshua, the leader who took the Israelites into the promised land. The name Jesus is the Greek form of Joshua.

In Acts one we read that the disciples asked Jesus, 'Lord are you at this time going to restore the kingdom to Israel?' He said to them: 'It is not for you to know the times and the dates the Father has set by his own authority ...' By their writings and the writings of Paul it is clear that they expected his return to be very soon. Perhaps If they were told that two thousand years later we would be still waiting and looking for his appearing they might have relaxed in their efforts to share the good news of the kingdom of God and perhaps lost their sense of urgency and just got on with their day jobs.

That message is still to be shared with a sense of urgency because none of us know how long we have – how much time we personally have. The writer of the letter to the Hebrews emphasised repeatedly the word 'Today' in the context of listening and acting on what you have learned. Before the Israelites came to the promised land they had been told the good news of where they were headed but they did not have the faith or obedience that others had so they did not enter that land. We, if we ignore the message and lack faith and are disobedient to our calling, can end up not entering that kingdom that is still ahead of us. But our time is short.

'We must pay the most careful attention to what

we have heard, so that we do not drift away … how shall we escape if we ignore so great a salvation,' the writer tells us in chapter two of Hebrews.

'But about that day or hour no-one knows, not even the angels in heaven, nor the Son, but only the Father. Be on guard, be alert, you do not know when that time will come. It's like a man going away: he leaves his house and puts his servants in charge, each with an assigned task, and tells the one at the door to keep watch. Therefore keep watch because you do not know when the owner of the house will come back – whether in the evening, or at midnight, or when the cock crows, or at dawn. If he comes suddenly, do not let him find you sleeping. What I say to you, I say to everyone: Watch.'

Mark 13:32-37

Part 16

A Change of Heart

erhaps it was with some frustration that Moses wrote to the tribes of Israel, 'Circumcise your hearts, and don't be stiff-necked any longer,' Deut 10:16.

A little before this heartfelt statement he had written, 'And now Israel, what does the Lord your God ask of you but to fear the Lord your God, to walk in obedience to him, to love him, to serve the Lord your God with all of your heart and with all of your soul, and to observe the Lord's commands and decrees that I am giving you today for your own good.' Deut 10:12-13.

Back in chapter four Moses writes, 'See, I have taught you decrees and laws as the Lord my God commanded me, so that you may follow them in the land you are entering to take possession of it. Observe them carefully, for this will show your wisdom and understanding to the nations who will hear about all these decrees and say. 'Surely this great nation is a wise and understanding people.' What other nation is so great as to have their gods near them the way the Lord our God is near us whenever we pray to him? And what other nation is so great as to have such righteous decrees and laws as this body of laws I am setting before you today?'

Great results are promised to Israel if they are obedient. Chapter 28 begins with God's promise, 'If you fully obey the Lord your God and carefully follow all his commands that I give you today, the Lord your God will set you high above all the nations on earth. All these blessings will come on you and accompany you if you obey the Lord your God:

> You will be blessed in the city and blessed in the country.
>
> The fruit of your womb will be blessed, and the crops of your land and the young of your livestock – the calves of your herds and the lambs of your flocks.
>
> Your basket and your kneading trough will be blessed.
>
> You will be blessed when you come in and blessed when you go out'

The blessings continue and cover every aspect of their lives. And they are also told what would happen if they were not obedient towards God – the exact opposite of the blessings – curses, for them, their health, their land, their produce, with the weather and their relationships with other nations.

What went wrong? They were human, just like us, and whenever there was a problem or difficulty they complained. Hebrews 3-4 makes it clear that it was unbelief that stopped them entering the promised land. They had received the good news. They had been liberated from slavery in Egypt, seen the sea parting to allow them to walk across on dry land, and been led by a pillar of fire during the night pillar of cloud during the day yet when difficulties came they criticised the leadership and questioned whether God was really with them. They lacked the faith to trust God when circumstances did not go the way they expected. How different would we have been?

'Understand then,' Moses told them in Deut 9:6-7, 'that it is not because of your righteousness that the Lord your God is giving you this good land to possess, for you are a stiff-necked people.

'Remember this and never forget how you aroused the anger of the Lord your God in the wilderness. From the day you left Egypt until you arrived here, you have been rebellious against the Lord.'

Exodus 15:24: 'So the people grumbled against Moses.'

" 16:2: 'In the desert the whole community grumbled against Moses and Aaron'

" 17:3-4 'But the people were thirsty for water there, and they grumbled against Moses. They said, 'Why did you bring us up out of Egypt to make us and our children and livestock die of thirst?' Then Moses cried out to the Lord, 'What am I to do with these people? They are almost ready to stone me.'

" 17:7b 'the Israelites quarrelled and because they tested The Lord saying, 'Is the Lord among us or not?'

Numbers 14:1-4 'That night all the members of the community raised their voices and wept aloud. All the Israelites grumbled against Moses and Aaron, and the whole assembly said to them, 'If only we had died in Egypt! Or in this wilderness! Why is the Lord bringing us to this land only to let us fall by the sword? Our wives and children will be taken as plunder. Wouldn't it be better for us to go back to Egypt? And they said to each other, 'We should chose a leader and go back to Egypt.'

Num 16:3 'They (253 leaders) came as a group to oppose Moses and Aaron and said to them, 'You have gone too far! The whole community is holy, every one of them, and the Lord is with them. Why then do you set yourselves above the Lord's assembly?'

Deut 31: 26-27 'Take this book of the law,' Moses told the Levites, who were the priests, shortly before his death, 'and place it beside the ark of the covenant of the Lord your God. There it will remain a witness against you. For I know how rebellious and stiff-necked you are. If you have been rebellious against the Lord while I am still alive and with you, how much more will you rebel after I die!... For I know that after my death you are sure to become utterly corrupt and turn from the way I have commanded you. In days to come, disaster will fall on you because you will do evil in the sight of the Lord and arouse his anger by what your hands have made.'

The biblical record charts their downward spiral into violence, corruption and idolatry.

With a similar frustration Jeremiah wrote, 'Circumcise yourselves to the Lord, circumcise your hearts, you people of Judah and inhabitants of Jerusalem ...' Jer 4:4.

Circumcision, along with the Levitical priesthood, the sacrificial system and the temple are now obsolete and finished, although Paul had difficulty, as well as other leaders, in convincing other Jewish Christians that circumcision was indeed not required. Some had taught that 'unless you are circumcised you cannot be saved'. These Pharisees turned Christian were convinced that 'the Gentiles must be circumcised and required them to keep the law of Moses', Acts 15:1, 5.

To the Roman Christians Paul wrote, 'A person is not a Jew who is one only outwardly, nor is circumcision merely outward and physical. No, a person is a Jew who is one inwardly; and circumcision is circumcision of the heart, by the spirit, not by the written code. Such a person's praise is not from other people, but from God' Rom 2:28-29.

In writing to the Corinthians Paul writes, 'Circumcision is nothing and uncircumcision is nothing. Keeping God's commands is what counts' 1Cor 7:19. To the Galatians he says, 'For in Christ Jesus neither circumcision nor uncircumcision has any value. The only thing that counts is faith expressing itself through love' 5:6.

Paul further explains the significance of this subject to the Ephesians, 'Remember that formerly you who were Gentiles by birth and called 'uncircumcised' by those who call themselves 'the circumcision' – remember that at that time you were separate from Christ, excluded from citizenship in Israel and foreigners to the covenants of the promise, without hope without God in the world. But now in Christ Jesus you who were once far away have been brought near by the blood of Christ.

'For he himself is our peace, who has made the two one and has destroyed the barrier, the dividing wall of hostility, by setting aside in his flesh the law with its commands and regulations. His purpose was to create in himself one new humanity out of the two, thus making peace, and in one body to reconcile both of them to God through the cross, by which he put to death their hostility' 2:11-16.

Paul encouraged the Corinthians in his second letter to them by saying, 'You show that you are a letter from Christ, the result of our ministry, written not with ink but with the Spirit of the living God, not on tablets of stone but on tablets of human hearts ...Now if the ministry that brought death, which was engraved in letters on stone, came with glory, so that the Israelites could not look steadily at the face of Moses because of its glory, transitory though it was, will not the ministry of the Spirit be even more glorious? If the ministry that brought condemnation was glorious, how much more glorious is the ministry that brings righteousness! For what was glorious has no glory now in comparison with the surpassing glory. And if what was transitory came with glory, how much greater is the glory of that which lasts!

Therefore since we have such a hope, we are very bold. We are not like Moses, who would put a veil over his face from preventing the Israelites from seeing the end of what was passing away. But their minds were made dull, for to this day the same veil remains when the old covenant is read. It has not been removed, because only in Christ is it taken away. Even to this day when Moses is read, a veil covers their hearts. But whenever anyone turns to the Lord, the veil is taken away. Now the Lord is the Spirit, and where the Spirit of the Lord is, there is freedom. And we all, who with unveiled faces reflect the Lord's glory, are being transformed into his image with ever-increasing glory, which comes from the Lord, who is the Spirit' 2Cor 3:3-18.

To the Colossians he wrote, 'Here there is no Gentile or Jew, circumcised or uncircumcised, barbarian, Scythian, slave or free, but Christ is all, and is in all' Col 3:11.

Ezekiel writes as one who was deported from Judah to the land of the Babylonians, 'I will give you a new heart and put a new spirit in you; I will remove from you your heart of stone and give you a heart of flesh. And I will put my spirit in you and move you to follow my decrees and be careful to keep my laws' 36:26-27.

We humans need a new heart – a new spirit, 'Rid yourselves of all the offences you have committed, and get a new heart and a new spirit. Why will you die, house of Israel? For I take no pleasure in the death of anyone, declares the Sovereign Lord. Repent and live! 18:31-32.

Describing a new covenant God says, through Jeremiah, 'This is the covenant that I will make with the house of Israel after that time. I will put my law in their minds and write it on their hearts. I will be their God and they will be my people' Jer 31:33.

'For the word of God is alive and active. Sharper than any double-edged sword, it penetrates even to dividing soul and spirit, joints and marrow; it judges the thoughts and attitudes of the heart. Nothing in all creation is hidden from God's sight. Everything is uncovered and laid bare before the eyes of him to whom we must give account' Heb 4;12-13.

The Jews at the time of Jesus had as little to do with Gentiles as possible. Peter said to Cornelius, a devout and God-fearing centurion, and those with him, 'you are well aware that it is against our law for a Jew to associate with Gentiles or visit them. But God has shown me that I should not call anyone impure or unclean' Acts 10:28. Peter now understood the vision that he had seen two days earlier when he had been shown creatures which he believed were not fit to eat being lowered to the ground and was told to kill and eat and Peter had replied that he had never eaten anything impure or unclean.

In Mark 7 Jesus exposes the teaching of man-made traditions as law, such as how and when to wash because the hair-splitting, legalistic and overly critical Pharisees had seen the disciples of Jesus eating without washing their hands – how shocking!

A little dust or dirt does not defile a person, as Jesus pointed out, but what can defile a person is what comes out from their heart. What a person eats and choses to drink does not defile them. Paul said to the Romans, 'Some consider one day more sacred than another, others consider every day alike. Everyone should be fully convinced in their own mind. Those who regard one day as special do so to the Lord. Those who eat meat do so to the Lord, for they give thanks to God, and those who abstain do so to the Lord and give thanks to the Lord ... Or why do you treat your brother or sister with contempt? For we will all stand before God's judgment seat ... therefore let us stop passing judgment on one another. Instead, make up your mind not to put any stumbling-block or obstacle in the way of a brother or sister. I am convinced, being fully persuaded in the Lord Jesus, that nothing is unclean in itself. But if anyone regards something as unclean, then for that person it is unclean. If your brother or sister is distressed because of what you eat, you are no longer acting in love. Do not by your eating destroy your brother or sister for whom Christ died.

Therefore do not let what you know is good be spoken of as evil. For the kingdom of God is not a matter of eating and drinking, but of righteousness, peace and joy in the Holy Spirit. Because anyone who serves Christ in this way is pleasing to God and receives human approval.

Let us make every effort to do what leads to peace and to mutual edification. Do not destroy the work of God for the sake of food. All food is clean, but it is wrong for a person to eat anything that causes someone else to stumble. It is better not to eat meat or drink wine or do anything else that will cause your brother or sister to fall.

So whatever you believe about these things keep between yourself and God' Rom 14:5-22a.

Colossians 2:16-17 says the same thing in a

different way. 'Do not let anyone judge you by what you eat and drink, or with regard to a religious festival, a new moon celebration or a sabbath day. These are a shadow of the things that were to come; the reality, however, is found in Christ.'

J.B. Phillips puts it this way: 'In view of these tremendous facts, don't let anyone worry you by criticising what you eat or drink, or what holy days you ought to observe, or bothering you over new moons or sabbaths. All these things have at most only a symbolic value: the solid fact is Christ.' While The Message has: 'So don't put up with anyone pressuring you in details of diet, worship services, or holy days. All those things are mere shadows cast before what was to come; the substance is Christ.'

It is not the outward performance of a Christian ritual that really counts, no matter which fellowship or denomination you belong to, but what is in your heart. All judgment belongs to God. He is judging his people now, 1Peter 4:17 and the rest of humanity will be judged after the thousand-year-reign of the Messiah on earth.

Part 17

Calling

S ome look at the plumage of a bird, or at the sky, or the diversity of seeds and what they produce and know in their hearts that there is a Creator who designed all life wonderfully.

But others are fully convinced by the teaching that all we see has gradually evolved over millions of years, yet, if the reproductive systems for each creature are not working perfectly there is no second generation. Some believe there is no God because of all the suffering that happens day after day and reason that if there was a God that suffering would stop, which would mean that all humans would not have a choice – they would have no will of their own.

Jesus knew that many, if not most, of the people listening to him would reject what he said. There would also be those who would respond positively, yet later, when persecution or trouble comes they fall away. Then there are the worries of life and the glamour of the world that can lead to a person to being unproductive in their Christian life. But there are those who listen and understand and become very productive with what they have.

The majority of those who heard Jesus speak not only didn't understand – they didn't want to understand. Light had come into their world but they preferred darkness because of the type of lives they led.

If people do not come to God it's due to a decision that they themselves make. God's calling has always, in one way or another, been with us but it is we who have hardened our hearts, just as the Israelites who were rescued from slavery had done.

'Brothers and sisters,' Paul wrote in Romans 10, 'my heart's desire and prayer to God for the Israelites is that they may be saved. For I can testify about them that they are zealous for God, but their zeal isn't based on knowledge. Since they didn't know the righteousness of God and sought to establish their own, they didn't submit to God's righteousness ...' Paul goes on to quote from Deuteronomy 30, showing his readers that the words of Moses are relevant to them, and us today. 'Now what I'm commanding today isn't too difficult for you or beyond your reach – it's not up in heaven ... nor is it beyond the sea ... no, the word is very near you, it's in your mouth and in your heart so that you may obey it.' Paul continues, 'That is, the message concerning faith that we proclaim; If you declare with your mouth, 'Jesus is Lord' and believe in your heart that God raised him from the dead, you will be saved. For it's with your heart that you believe and are justified, and it's with your mouth that you profess your faith and are saved … for there's no difference between Jew and Gentile – the same Lord is Lord of all and richly blesses all who call on him, for' quoting Joel 2:32, 'Everyone who calls on the name of the Lord will be saved,'

'How, then, can they call on the one they have not believed in? And how can they believe in the one of whom they haven't heard? And how can they hear without someone preaching to them? And how can anyone preach unless they're sent? As it's written: 'How beautiful are the feet of those who bring good news' Isa 52:7.

'But not all the Israelites accepted the good news. For Isaiah says, 'Lord, who has believed our message?' Isa 53:1. Consequently, faith comes from hearing the message, and the message is heard through the word about Christ. But I ask: did they not hear? Of course they did'. Paul then quotes verse 4 from Psalm 19, let's read it from verse 1, 'The heavens declare the glory of God; the skies *proclaim* the work of his hands. Day after day they pour forth *speech*; night after night they display knowledge. They have no speech; they use no words; no sound is heard from them. Yet their *voice* has gone out into all the earth, their *words* to the ends of the world'.

'Again I ask: did Israel not understand? First, Moses says, I'll make you envious by those who are not a nation; I'll make you angry by a nation that has no understanding' Deut 32:21.

And Isaiah boldly says, 'I was found by those who didn't seek me; I revealed myself to those who didn't ask for me' Isa 65:1.

But concerning Israel he says, 'All day long I've held out my hands to a disobedient and obstinate people' Isa 65:2.

A little further on Paul writes, 'Consider therefor the kindness and sternness of God: sternness to those who fell (Israel), but kindness to you (Gentiles), provided that you continue in his kindness. Otherwise, you also will be cut off. And if they don't persist in unbelief, they'll be grafted in, for God is able to graft them in again' Rom 11:22-23.

There was a time when many of Jesus' followers left him because they couldn't accept what he was saying. He asked those still with him,

'You don't want to leave too, do you? They had a choice – no-one was making them stay and what Jesus had just been saying was hard to take, let alone understand – he had been taking about eating his flesh and drinking his blood, which to many sounded like cannibalism.

The disciples had no idea what he was talking about, nevertheless, Peter said to Jesus, 'Lord, to whom shall we go? You have the words of eternal life – we've come to believe and know that you are the Holy One of God' John 6:66-69.

In verse 44 of that chapter Jesus said, 'No-one can come to me unless the Father who sent me draws them …' Jesus repeats himself in verse 65, 'This is why I told you that no-one can come to me unless the Father has enabled them.'

These statements came because people were being critical as well as objecting to what Jesus was saying to them. God's call goes out to all but only a few respond positively to it. This world is a war zone, with the forces of good fighting the forces of evil. Sometimes the dragon can hinder God's purposes. God's will is that everyone is saved, II Peter 3:9, I Tim 2:4. But not everyone chooses to answer the call and be saved – it's our decision to answer God's call or not, and thus determine our own eternal fate.

In the example of prayer that Jesus gave us, we read; 'your kingdom come, your will be done,' we're to ask this because God's kingdom isn't here and his will isn't always done. There are competing wills here on earth – my will, your will, the many wills of those around us. It was the will of well-known leaders in church history that if you disagreed with them and wrote about it or supported those who spoke out against their teachings that you would be tried in court and if found to be guilty you would be put to death – that was their will, not God's. Their spiritual descendants can no longer hand those they considered as heretics over to the civil authorities for execution but they do speak much of such people suffering in hell for an eternity.

The will of many is to steal, kill and destroy, which is the dragon's will, so we are encouraged to pray not only for God's kingdom to come but also for his will to be done – in our lives as well as others.

Calvinists might say that God cannot be God unless He controls everything – in other words, everything that happens is God's will. God doesn't want to control everything that people do – He wants them to see and hear the truth – to repent and move from darkness to light – to give them support and that they will make wise choices themselves.

God hates all evil, cruelty and lies and the dragon is the father of lies.

Calvinists teach that before the creation of the world God foreknew who was to be given eternal life and who was condemned to eternal death. Their was no choice in it – if you repented, that was God's will before you were born and it was unconditional. If you refused to repent, that also was determined by God long before you were born.

But God invites us to come to him. We do have a choice. The people of Israel were given a choice to obey God and receive incredible blessings or refuse and bring on themselves ruin.

On the eighth and last day of the Feast of Tabernacles held in the seventh month in the year, which was a great celebration, remembering where they had been and where they were now. Jesus stood and said in a loud voice, 'Let anyone who is thirsty come to me and drink. Whoever believes in me, as scripture has said, rivers of living waters will flow from within them' … On hearing these words, some of the people said, 'Surely this man is the Prophet', others said 'he's the Messiah'. Still others asked 'How can the Messiah come from Galilee? Doesn't scripture say that the Messiah will come from David's descendants and from Bethlehem, the town where David lived? Thus the people were divided because of Jesus. Some wanted to seize him, but no-one laid a hand on him. John 7: 37-44.

All sorts of reactions towards Jesus; most of which were negative but we read that after Peter's speech on the day of Pentecost about three thousand people were added to the church. From what these people saw and felt when Jesus died on the cross, and that many of them were those who 'beat their breasts and went away (Luke 23:48, Zech 12:10), and what they heard from Peter, convinced them of their guilt and sin, and their lives were changed from that moment on. God, through their experience and the words of Peter, was calling them. How we respond to God's call is our choice and decision.

'Here I am. I stand at the door and knock. If anyone hears my voice and opens the door, I will come in and eat with them, and they with me'

Rev 3:20

Part 18

Elementary Teachings

*G*od:

Gen 1:1 – Rev 22:21, Exo 34:5-7, Deut 4:7-8, Psa 19, Psa 86:10, John 17:3, Acts 5:29, Phil 2:9-11, 1Pet 5:6-7, Heb 4:13, 1John 4:15-16, 1Tim 2:1-6, Rev 21:3-4.

Jesus Christ:

Or Joshua the Anointed One. Isa 7:14. A descendent of king David. Born by the power of God, Luke 1:31-33. The second Adam, as Paul called him, 1Cor 15:45. He is our atoning sacrifice, Rom 5:6-8, 1John 2:2, 4:10. Through him we are reconciled to God, Rom 5:9-11, II Cor 5:18, 1Pet 3:18, 1John 3:16. He is our great high priest and Judge, Heb 4:14, Acts 10:42-43.

His death and resurrection:

Jesus died on the cross at about 3pm on the fourth day of the week (Wednesday) and rose three days and three nights later – late afternoon as the sun was setting on the seventh day of the week (Saturday).

The Gospel:

The core message of Jesus was the Kingdom of God. Matt 6:10, 20:21, Mark 1:14, Mark 14:2, Luke 8:1, 9:2, 13:28, 17:20, 18:25, 19:11, 22:16, 30, 23:51, John 3:5, 18:36, Acts 1:6, 19:8, 28:23, 31, 1Cor 15:50, Gal 5:21, Eph 5:5, Col 4:11, II Thes 1:5, Rev 3:12, 12:10.

Baptism:

Matt 3:13-15, Mark 1:4, Luke 3:3, 7:29, John 3:22, Acts 2:36-38, 10:47-48, 16:31-33, Rom 6:4, Eph 4;5, Col 2:12, 1Pet 3:21.

The First Resurrection:

Matt 22:29-32, Luke 19:12-17, John 5:28, Acts 24:15,21, Rev 20:4.

The Second Resurrection:

Dan 12:2-4, Mal 4:1-3, John 5:28-29, Rev 20:5, 11-15.

'Let us move beyond the elementary teachings about Christ and be taken forward to maturity'

Hebrews 6:1

'Grow in the grace and knowledge of
our Lord and Saviour Jesus Christ. To
him be glory both now and forever'

II Peter 3:18

It was right at the end of the film, Randolph Scott was standing over Joel McCrea who was close to death following a climactic gunfight where the two of them walked towards the three Hammond brothers, armed men who were intent on killing them. Guns were blazing – all were being hit by bullets, Scott was wounded but McCrea took too many and was on the ground. When the firing stopped and the villains dead they considered their wounds. There had been a rift between the two but now Scott promised McCrea that the gold shipment would get to where it belonged. Knowing that his friend was about to die, Scott, fighting back his tears, said to McCrea, 'I'll see you later.' And walked away while McCrea lowered his head to the ground.

Part 19

Imagine

That 'I'll see you later' from the 1962 Western, 'Ride The High Country' had become an affectionate expression between Derek and Helen, an elderly couple who knew that one day they'd be saying it for the last time, and now that time had come. They both understood that he was very close to death and he was slipping in and out of consciousness, so they said it to each other – there might not be another time when it would be possible. They loved each other and both believed Christ would return, when? They had no idea, but whenever it happened they'll see each other again. She stayed by his side long after he was no longer able to respond in any way.

He felt completely weakened by his condition and in what was to be the last time, he opened his eyes and saw her, he wanted to smile, he wanted to tell her he wasn't afraid, that he was looking forward to seeing his Saviour, but he couldn't. Sleep was coming, it was getting dark, there was … nothing … he woke … his eyes were wide open and he looked around but he was no longer laying down – he was, to his amazement, standing outside, the sky seemed low and dark and threatening. The sun couldn't be seen and there was a reddish hue to the darkness. He became aware of something else …

Energy, strength, power. He'd never felt anything like this before, it was as if he had nuclear power within himself and had no idea where he was … a single bright light came towards him and as it got closer he saw what looked like a man, but not a human … it spoke, 'the time has come, we must join the others.' Immediately the ground was falling away. They were ascending at great speed but he felt no wind resistance or change in the air pressure and when he looked around he saw other lights heading in the same direction like bullets of laser lights, all heading upwards. There were more than he could count. He raised his head and looked up, his mouth opened, there were millions of these lights and they were coming down towards them.

Somehow those who were descending slowed down, so did he and all the other lights – they came together and if he were still a human his eyes wouldn't have been able to look at what was all round him. The light was indescribable and he couldn't hold back a cry of joy as he took in what he was a part of. Without anything needing to be said all of them turned their faces to earth.

Back on the ground the military forces of many nations were hurriedly training their weapons skywards at this dreadful threat to their existence that was fast approaching. Their weapons had no effect at all and they were defenceless against this alien attack. The invading force used light itself as a weapon – its blazing heat destroyed everything it fell on. They were unstoppable and were now landing amidst blackened and smoking devastation. The resistance was eradicated. Those who fought against them were dead. Now this alien force was in control. Derek knew that he was part of this all-conquering army and his mental capacity was no longer limited as it was as a human. He now knew more than he could ever have known as a flesh and blood man.

He saw all this and remembered that this violent take-over was long ago foretold to happen and that it would be aggressively resisted yet fail in its attempt to stop this overwhelming power from another place. All these beings of light were now looking in the same direction – towards the centre at a source of light that was even greater than their own. He moved towards it and grasped that commands were being given that everyone understood as though they'd heard them before. He moved even closer and then their eyes met – he wanted to say something but nothing came out, no eyes were like his, the greater light spoke, 'Well done, you've been faithful with just a small amount – I'll put you in charge of many things. Come and share my happiness.' He smiled as he spoke and for some reason Derek turned and saw Helen with tears running down her cheeks while beaming with a great grin, 'I told you I'd see you later.' She too was full of light and power. There was much to do, and they had the time and capability to do it, they would not taste death again, There was a world to restore and heal and there were precious humans to teach and lead, it was the first day of the new age. The King had returned.

He who was seated on the throne said, 'I am making everything new' Then he said, 'Write this down, for these words are trustworthy and true.'

Revelation 21:5

Acknowledgements

L ots of writers, lots of books, some of which I now no longer have. I have added the names of those authors whose books I still have in the sections where I have used their works which I have heavily leaned on. As well as these there has been the TNIV & the Harper Collins Study Bible & Cruden's Concordance & Lutterworth's Dictionary of the Bible plus the REV Bible App from the Spirit & Truth Fellowship International for which I am very grateful for having, even though I may differ on some points with them, I would highly recommend this app to all bible students of all ages.

Printed in the United States
by Baker & Taylor Publisher Services